The Complete Poems of

Emily Dickinson

Published by Pantianos Classics

ISBN-13: 978-1540408013

First published in 1924

A map of Amhurst, Massachusetts, dating to 1886

The old chapel in Amhurst, Massachusetts

Emily Dickenson in 1847, aged 16

Contents

Poems of Emily Dickenson - First Series

Preface

The verses of Emily Dickinson belong emphatically to what Emerson long since called "the Poetry of the Portfolio,"—something produced absolutely without the thought of publication, and solely by way of expression of the writer's own mind. Such verse must inevitably forfeit whatever advantage lies in the discipline of public criticism and the enforced conformity to accepted ways. On the other hand, it may often gain something through the habit of freedom and the unconventional utterance of daring thoughts. In the case of the present author, there was absolutely no choice in the matter; she must write thus, or not at all. A recluse by temperament and habit, literally spending years without setting her foot beyond the doorstep, and many more years during which her walks were strictly limited to her father's grounds, she habitually concealed her mind, like her person, from all but a very few friends; and it was with great difficulty that she was persuaded to print, during her lifetime, three or four poems. Yet she wrote verses in great abundance; and though brought curiously indifferent to all conventional rules, had yet a rigorous literary standard of her own, and often altered a word many times to suit an ear which had its own tenacious fastidiousness.

Miss Dickinson was born in Amherst, Mass., Dec. 10, 1830, and died there May 15, 1886. Her father, Hon. Edward Dickinson, was the leading lawyer of Amherst, and was treasurer of the well-known college there situated. It was his custom once a year to hold a large reception at his house, attended by all the families connected with the institution and by the leading people of the town. On these occasions his daughter Emily emerged from her wonted retirement and did her part as gracious hostess; nor would any one have known from her manner, I have been told, that this was not a daily occurrence. The annual occasion once past, she withdrew again into her seclusion, and except for a very few friends was as invisible to the world as if she had dwelt in a nunnery. For myself, although I had corresponded with her for many years, I saw her but twice face to face, and brought away the impression of something as unique and remote as Undine or Mignon or Thekla.

This selection from her poems is published to meet the desire of her personal friends, and especially of her surviving sister. It is believed that the thoughtful reader will find in these pages a quality more suggestive of the poetry of William Blake than of anything to be elsewhere found,— flashes of wholly original and profound insight into nature and life; words and phrases exhibiting an extraordinary vividness of descriptive and imaginative power, yet often set in a seemingly whimsical or even rugged frame. They are here published as they were written, with very few and superficial changes; although it is fair to say that the titles have been assigned, almost invariably, by the editors. In many cases these verses will seem to the reader like poetry torn up by the roots, with rain and dew and earth still clinging to them, giving a freshness and a fragrance not otherwise to be conveyed. In other cases, as in the few poems of shipwreck or of mental conflict, we can only wonder at the gift of vivid imagination by which this recluse woman can delineate, by a few touches, the very crises of physical or mental struggle. And sometimes again we catch glimpses of a lyric strain, sustained perhaps but for a line or two at a time, and making the reader regret its sudden cessation. But the main quality of these poems is that of extraordinary grasp and insight, uttered with an uneven vigor sometimes exasperating, seemingly wayward, but really unsought and inevitable. After all, when a thought takes one's breath away, a lesson on grammar seems an impertinence. As Ruskin wrote in his earlier and better days, "No weight nor mass nor beauty of execution can outweigh one grain or fragment of thought."

- Thomas Wentworth Higginson

This is my letter to the world,
That never wrote to me, —
The simple news that Nature told,
With tender majesty.

Her message is committed
To hands I cannot see;
For love of her, sweet countrymen,
Judge tenderly of me!

I. Life.

I - SUCCESS

[Published in "A Masque of Poets"
at the request of "H.H.," the
author's
fellow-townswoman and friend.]

Success is counted sweetest
By those who ne'er succeed.
To comprehend a nectar
Requires sorest need.

Not one of all the purple host
Who took the flag to-day
Can tell the definition,
So clear, of victory,

As he, defeated, dying,
On whose forbidden ear
The distant strains of triumph
Break, agonized and clear!

II.

Our share of night to bear,
Our share of morning,
Our blank in bliss to fill,
Our blank in scorning.

Here a star, and there a star,
Some lose their way.
Here a mist, and there a mist,
Afterwards — day!

III - Rouge Et Noir

Soul, wilt thou toss again?

By just such a hazard
Hundreds have lost, indeed,
But tens have won an all.

Angels' breathless ballot
Lingers to record thee;
Imps in eager caucus
Raffle for my soul.

IV - Rouge Gagne

'T is so much joy! 'T is so much
joy!
If I should fail, what poverty!
And yet, as poor as I
Have ventured all upon a throw;
Have gained! Yes! Hesitated so
This side the victory!

Life is but life, and death but
death!
Bliss is but bliss, and breath but
breath!
And if, indeed, I fail,
At least to know the worst is
sweet.
Defeat means nothing but defeat,
No drearier can prevail!

And if I gain, — oh, gun at sea,
Oh, bells that in the steeples be,
At first repeat it slow!
For heaven is a different thing
Conjectured, and waked sudden
in,
And might o'erwhelm me so!

V.

Glee! The great storm is over!
Four have recovered the land;
Forty gone down together
Into the boiling sand.

Ring, for the scant salvation!
Toll, for the bonnie souls, —
Neighbor and friend and
bridegroom,
Spinning upon the shoals!

How they will tell the shipwreck
When winter shakes the door,
Till the children ask, "But the
forty?
Did they come back no more?"

Then a silence suffuses the story,
And a softness the teller's eye;
And the children no further
question,
And only the waves reply.

VI.

If I can stop one heart from
breaking,
I shall not live in vain;
If I can ease one life the aching,
Or cool one pain,
Or help one fainting robin
Unto his nest again,
I shall not live in vain.

VII - Almost!

Within my reach!
I could have touched!
I might have chanced that way!
Soft sauntered through the village,
Sauntered as soft away!
So unsuspected violets
Within the fields lie low,
Too late for striving fingers
That passed, an hour ago.

VIII.

A wounded deer leaps highest,
I've heard the hunter tell;
'T is but the ecstasy of death,
And then the brake is still.

The smitten rock that gushes,
The trampled steel that springs;
A cheek is always redder
Just where the hectic stings!

Mirth is the mail of anguish,
In which it cautions arm,
Lest anybody spy the blood
And "You're hurt" exclaim!

IX.

The heart asks pleasure first,
And then, excuse from pain;
And then, those little anodynes
That deaden suffering;

And then, to go to sleep;
And then, if it should be
The will of its Inquisitor,
The liberty to die.

X - In a Library.

A precious, mouldering pleasure 't
is
To meet an antique book,
In just the dress his century wore;
A privilege, I think,

His venerable hand to take,
And warming in our own,
A passage back, or two, to make
To times when he was young.

His quaint opinions to inspect,
His knowledge to unfold
On what concerns our mutual
mind,
The literature of old;

What interested scholars most,
What competitions ran
When Plato was a certainty.
And Sophocles a man;

When Sappho was a living girl,
And Beatrice wore
The gown that Dante deified.
Facts, centuries before,

He traverses familiar,
As one should come to town
And tell you all your dreams were
true;
He lived where dreams were
sown.

His presence is enchantment,
You beg him not to go;
Old volumes shake their vellum
heads
And tantalize, just so.

XI.

Much madness is divinest sense
To a discerning eye;
Much sense the starkest madness.
'T is the majority
In this, as all, prevails.
Assent, and you are sane;
Demur, — you're straightway
dangerous,
And handled with a chain.

XII.

I asked no other thing,
No other was denied.
I offered Being for it;
The mighty merchant smiled.

Brazil? He twirled a button,
Without a glance my way:
"But, madam, is there nothing else
That we can show to-day?"

XIII - Exclusion

The soul selects her own society,
Then shuts the door;
On her divine majority
Obtrude no more.

Unmoved, she notes the chariot's
pausing
At her low gate;
Unmoved, an emperor is kneeling
Upon her mat.

I've known her from an ample
nation

Choose one;
Then close the valves of her attention
Like stone.

XIV - The Secret

Some things that fly there be, —
Birds, hours, the bumble-bee:
Of these no elegy.

Some things that stay there be, —
Grief, hills, eternity:
Nor this behooveth me.

There are, that resting, rise.
Can I expound the skies?
How still the riddle lies!

XV - The Lonely House

I know some lonely houses off the road
A robber 'd like the look of, —
Wooden barred,
And windows hanging low,
Inviting to
A portico,
Where two could creep:
One hand the tools,
The other peep
To make sure all's asleep.
Old-fashioned eyes,
Not easy to surprise!

How orderly the kitchen 'd look by night,
With just a clock, —
But they could gag the tick,

And mice won't bark;
And so the walls don't tell,
None will.

A pair of spectacles ajar just stir —
An almanac's aware.
Was it the mat winked,
Or a nervous star?
The moon slides down the stair
To see who's there.

There's plunder, — where?
Tankard, or spoon,
Earring, or stone,
A watch, some ancient brooch
To match the grandmamma,
Staid sleeping there.
Day rattles, too,
Stealth's slow;
The sun has got as far
As the third sycamore.
Screams chanticleer,
"Who's there?"
And echoes, trains away,
Sneer — "Where?"
While the old couple, just astir,
Fancy the sunrise left the door ajar!

XVI.

To fight aloud is very brave,
But gallanter, I know,
Who charge within the bosom,
The cavalry of woe.

Who win, and nations do not see,
Who fall, and none observe,
Whose dying eyes no country
Regards with patriot love.

We trust, in plumed procession,
For such the angels go,
Rank after rank, with even feet
And uniforms of snow.

XVII - Dawn

When night is almost done,
And sunrise grows so near
That we can touch the spaces,
It 's time to smooth the hair

And get the dimples ready,
And wonder we could care
For that old faded midnight
That frightened but an hour.

XVIII - The Book of Martyrs

Read, sweet, how others strove,
Till we are stouter;
What they renounced,
Till we are less afraid;
How many times they bore
The faithful witness,
Till we are helped,
As if a kingdom cared!

Read then of faith
That shone above the fagot;
Clear strains of hymn
The river could not drown;
Brave names of men
And celestial women,
Passed out of record
Into renown!

XIX - The Mystery of Pain

Pain has an element of blank;
It cannot recollect

When it began, or if there were
A day when it was not.

It has no future but itself,
Its infinite realms contain
Its past, enlightened to perceive
New periods of pain.

XX.

I taste a liquor never brewed,
From tankards scooped in pearl;
Not all the vats upon the Rhine
Yield such an alcohol!

Inebriate of air am I,
And debauchee of dew,
Reeling, through endless summer
days,
From inns of molten blue.

When landlords turn the drunken
bee
Out of the foxglove's door,
When butterflies renounce their
drams,
I shall but drink the more!

Till seraphs swing their snowy
hats,
And saints to windows run,
To see the little tippler
Leaning against the sun!

XXI - A Book

He ate and drank the precious
words,
His spirit grew robust;

13

He knew no more that he was
poor,
Nor that his frame was dust.
He danced along the dingy days,
And this bequest of wings
Was but a book. What liberty
A loosened spirit brings!

XXII.

I had no time to hate, because
The grave would hinder me,
And life was not so ample I
Could finish enmity.

Nor had I time to love; but since
Some industry must be,
The little toil of love, I thought,
Was large enough for me.

XXIII - Unreturning

'T was such a little, little boat
That toddled down the bay!
'T was such a gallant, gallant sea
That beckoned it away!

'T was such a greedy, greedy wave
That licked it from the coast;
Nor ever guessed the stately sails
My little craft was lost!

XXIV.

Whether my bark went down at
sea,
Whether she met with gales,
Whether to isles enchanted
She bent her docile sails;

By what mystic mooring
She is held to-day, —
This is the errand of the eye
Out upon the bay.

XXV.

Belshazzar had a letter, —
He never had but one;
Belshazzar's correspondent
Concluded and begun
In that immortal copy
The conscience of us all
Can read without its glasses
On revelation's wall.

XXVI.

The brain within its groove
Runs evenly and true;
But let a splinter swerve,
'T were easier for you
To put the water back
When floods have slit the hills,
And scooped a turnpike for
themselves,
And blotted out the mills!

II. Love

I - Mine

Mine by the right of the white
election!
Mine by the royal seal!
Mine by the sign in the scarlet
prison
Bars cannot conceal!

Mine, here in vision and in veto!
Mine, by the grave's repeal
Titled, confirmed, — delirious
charter!
Mine, while the ages steal!

II - Bequest

You left me, sweet, two legacies,
—
A legacy of love
A Heavenly Father would content,
Had He the offer of;

You left me boundaries of pain
Capacious as the sea,
Between eternity and time,
Your consciousness and me.

III.

Alter? When the hills do.
Falter? When the sun
Question if his glory
Be the perfect one.

Surfeit? When the daffodil

Doth of the dew:
Even as herself, O friend!
I will of you!

IV - Suspense

Elysium is as far as to
The very nearest room,
If in that room a friend await
Felicity or doom.

What fortitude the soul contains,
That it can so endure
The accent of a coming foot,
The opening of a door!

V - Surrender

Doubt me, my dim companion!
Why, God would be content
With but a fraction of the love
Poured thee without a stint.
The whole of me, forever,
What more the woman can, —
Say quick, that I may dower thee
With last delight I own!

It cannot be my spirit,
For that was thine before;
I ceded all of dust I knew, —
What opulence the more
Had I, a humble maiden,
Whose farthest of degree
Was that she might,
Some distant heaven,
Dwell timidly with thee!

VI.

If you were coming in the fall,
I'd brush the summer by
With half a smile and half a spurn,
As housewives do a fly.

If I could see you in a year,
I'd wind the months in balls,
And put them each in separate
drawers,
Until their time befalls.

If only centuries delayed,
I'd count them on my hand,
Subtracting till my fingers
dropped
Into Van Diemen's land.

If certain, when this life was out,
That yours and mine should be,
I'd toss it yonder like a rind,
And taste eternity.

But now, all ignorant of the length
Of time's uncertain wing,
It goads me, like the goblin bee,
That will not state its sting.

VII - With a Flower

I hide myself within my flower,
That wearing on your breast,
You, unsuspecting, wear me too —
And angels know the rest.

I hide myself within my flower,
That, fading from your vase,
You, unsuspecting, feel for me
Almost a loneliness.

VIII - Proof

That I did always love,
I bring thee proof:
That till I loved
I did not love enough.

That I shall love alway,
I offer thee
That love is life,
And life hath immortality.

This, dost thou doubt, sweet?
Then have I
Nothing to show
But Calvary.

IX.

Have you got a brook in your little
heart,
Where bashful flowers blow,
And blushing birds go down to
drink,
And shadows tremble so?

And nobody knows, so still it
flows,
That any brook is there;
And yet your little draught of life
Is daily drunken there.

Then look out for the little brook
in March,
When the rivers overflow,
And the snows come hurrying
from the hills,
And the bridges often go.

And later, in August it may be,

When the meadows parching lie,
Beware, lest this little brook of life
Some burning noon go dry!

X - Transplanted

As if some little Arctic flower,
Upon the polar hem,
Went wandering down the
latitudes,
Until it puzzled came
To continents of summer,
To firmaments of sun,
To strange, bright crowds of
flowers,
And birds of foreign tongue!
I say, as if this little flower
To Eden wandered in —
What then? Why, nothing, only,
Your inference therefrom!

XI - The Outlet

My river runs to thee:
Blue sea, wilt welcome me?

My river waits reply.
Oh sea, look graciously!

I'll fetch thee brooks
From spotted nooks, —

Say, sea,
Take me!

XII - In Vain

I cannot live with you,
It would be life,

And life is over there
Behind the shelf

The sexton keeps the key to,
Putting up
Our life, his porcelain,
Like a cup

Discarded of the housewife,
Quaint or broken;
A newer Sevres pleases,
Old ones crack.

I could not die with you,
For one must wait
To shut the other's gaze down, —
You could not.

And I, could I stand by
And see you freeze,
Without my right of frost,
Death's privilege?

Nor could I rise with you,
Because your face
Would put out Jesus',
That new grace

Glow plain and foreign
On my homesick eye,
Except that you, than he
Shone closer by.

They'd judge us — how?
For you served Heaven, you know,
Or sought to;
I could not,

Because you saturated sight,
And I had no more eyes
For sordid excellence

As Paradise.

And were you lost, I would be,
Though my name
Rang loudest
On the heavenly fame.
And were you saved,
And I condemned to be
Where you were not,
That self were hell to me.

So we must keep apart,
You there, I here,
With just the door ajar
That oceans are,
And prayer,
And that pale sustenance,
Despair!

XIII - Renunciation

First page of Renunciation Second
page of Renunciation Third page
of Renunciation Fourth page of
Renunciation

There came a day at summer's full
Entirely for me;
I thought that such were for the
saints,
Where revelations be.

The sun, as common, went abroad,
The flowers, accustomed, blew,
As if no soul the solstice passed
That maketh all things new.

The time was scarce profaned by
speech;
The symbol of a word
Was needless, as at sacrament
The wardrobe of our Lord.

Each was to each the sealed
church,
Permitted to commune this time,
Lest we too awkward show
At supper of the Lamb.

The hours slid fast, as hours will,
Clutched tight by greedy hands;
So faces on two decks look back,
Bound to opposing lands.

And so, when all the time had
failed,
Without external sound,
Each bound the other's crucifix,
We gave no other bond.

Sufficient troth that we shall rise
—
Deposed, at length, the grave —
To that new marriage, justified
Through Calvaries of Love!

XIV - Love's Baptism

I'm ceded, I've stopped being
theirs;
The name they dropped upon my
face
With water, in the country church,
Is finished using now,
And they can put it with my dolls,
My childhood, and the string of
spools
I've finished threading too.

Baptized before without the choice,
But this time consciously, of grace
Unto supremest name,
Called to my full, the crescent dropped,
Existence's whole arc filled up
With one small diadem.

My second rank, too small the first,
Crowned, crowing on my father's breast,
A half unconscious queen;
But this time, adequate, erect,
With will to choose or to reject.
And I choose — just a throne.

XV - Resurrection

'T was a long parting, but the time
For interview had come;
Before the judgment-seat of God,
The last and second time

These fleshless lovers met,
A heaven in a gaze,
A heaven of heavens, the privilege
Of one another's eyes.

No lifetime set on them,
Apparelled as the new
Unborn, except they had beheld,
Born everlasting now.

Was bridal e'er like this?
A paradise, the host,
And cherubim and seraphim
The most familiar guest.

XVI - Apocalypse

I'm wife; I've finished that,
That other state;
I'm Czar, I'm woman now:
It's safer so.

How odd the girl's life looks
Behind this soft eclipse!
I think that earth seems so
To those in heaven now.

This being comfort, then
That other kind was pain;
But why compare?
I'm wife! stop there!

XVII - The Wife

She rose to his requirement, dropped
The playthings of her life
To take the honorable work
Of woman and of wife.

If aught she missed in her new day
Of amplitude, or awe,
Or first prospective, or the gold
In using wore away,

It lay unmentioned, as the sea
Develops pearl and weed,
But only to himself is known
The fathoms they abide.

XVIII - Apotheosis

Come slowly, Eden!
Lips unused to thee,

Bashful, sip thy jasmines,
As the fainting bee,

Reaching late his flower,
Round her chamber hums,
Counts his nectars — enters,
And is lost in balms!

III. Nature

I.

New feet within my garden go,
New fingers stir the sod;
A troubadour upon the elm
Betrays the solitude.

New children play upon the green,
New weary sleep below;
And still the pensive spring
returns,
And still the punctual snow!

II - May-Flower

Pink, small, and punctual,
Aromatic, low,
Covert in April,
Candid in May,

Dear to the moss,
Known by the knoll,
Next to the robin
In every human soul.

Bold little beauty,
Bedecked with thee,
Nature forswears
Antiquity.

III - Why?

The murmur of a bee
A witchcraft yieldeth me.
If any ask me why,
'T were easier to die

Than tell.

The red upon the hill
Taketh away my will;
If anybody sneer,
Take care, for God is here,
That's all.

The breaking of the day
Addeth to my degree;
If any ask me how,
Artist, who drew me so,
Must tell!

IV.

Perhaps you'd like to buy a
flower?
But I could never sell.
If you would like to borrow
Until the daffodil

Unties her yellow bonnet
Beneath the village door,
Until the bees, from clover rows
Their hock and sherry draw,

Why, I will lend until just then,
But not an hour more!

V.

The pedigree of honey
Does not concern the bee;
A clover, any time, to him
Is aristocracy.

VI - A Service Of Song

Some keep the Sabbath going to
church;
I keep it staying at home,
With a bobolink for a chorister,
And an orchard for a dome.

Some keep the Sabbath in
surplice;
I just wear my wings,
And instead of tolling the bell for
church,
Our little sexton sings.

God preaches, — a noted
clergyman, —
And the sermon is never long;
So instead of getting to heaven at
last,
I'm going all along!

VII.

The bee is not afraid of me,
I know the butterfly;
The pretty people in the woods
Receive me cordially.

The brooks laugh louder when I
come,
The breezes madder play.
Wherefore, mine eyes, thy silver
mists?
Wherefore, O summer's day?

VIII - Summer's Armies

Some rainbow coming from the
fair!

Some vision of the world
Cashmere
I confidently see!
Or else a peacock's purple train,
Feather by feather, on the plain
Fritters itself away!

The dreamy butterflies bestir,
Lethargic pools resume the whir
Of last year's sundered tune.
From some old fortress on the sun
Baronial bees march, one by one,
In murmuring platoon!

The robins stand as thick to-day
As flakes of snow stood yesterday,
On fence and roof and twig.
The orchis binds her feather on
For her old lover, Don the Sun,
Revisiting the bog!

Without commander, countless,
still,
The regiment of wood and hill
In bright detachment stand.
Behold! Whose multitudes are
these?
The children of whose turbaned
seas,
Or what Circassian land?

IX - The Grass

The grass so little has to do, —
A sphere of simple green,
With only butterflies to brood,
And bees to entertain,

And stir all day to pretty tunes
The breezes fetch along,

And hold the sunshine in its lap
And bow to everything;

And thread the dews all night, like
pearls,
And make itself so fine, —
A duchess were too common
For such a noticing.

And even when it dies, to pass
In odors so divine,
As lowly spices gone to sleep,
Or amulets of pine.

And then to dwell in sovereign
barns,
And dream the days away, —
The grass so little has to do,
I wish I were the hay!

X.

A little road not made of man,
Enabled of the eye,
Accessible to thill of bee,
Or cart of butterfly.

If town it have, beyond itself,
'T is that I cannot say;
I only sigh, — no vehicle
Bears me along that way.

XI - Summer Shower

A drop fell on the apple tree,
Another on the roof;
A half a dozen kissed the eaves,
And made the gables laugh.

A few went out to help the brook,
That went to help the sea.
Myself conjectured, Were they
pearls,
What necklaces could be!

The dust replaced in hoisted
roads,
The birds jocoser sung;
The sunshine threw his hat away,
The orchards spangles hung.

The breezes brought dejected
lutes,
And bathed them in the glee;
The East put out a single flag,
And signed the fete away.

XII - Psalm of the Day

A something in a summer's day,
As slow her flambeaux burn away,
Which solemnizes me.

A something in a summer's noon,
—
An azure depth, a wordless tune,
Transcending ecstasy.

And still within a summer's night
A something so transporting
bright,
I clap my hands to see;

Then veil my too inspecting face,
Lest such a subtle, shimmering
grace
Flutter too far for me.

The wizard-fingers never rest,

The purple brook within the
breast
Still chafes its narrow bed;

Still rears the East her amber flag,
Guides still the sun along the crag
His caravan of red,

Like flowers that heard the tale of
dews,
But never deemed the dripping
prize
Awaited their low brows;

Or bees, that thought the
summer's name
Some rumor of delirium
No summer could for them;

Or Arctic creature, dimly stirred
By tropic hint, — some travelled
bird
Imported to the wood;

Or wind's bright signal to the ear,
Making that homely and severe,
Contented, known, before

The heaven unexpected came,
To lives that thought their
worshipping
A too presumptuous psalm.

XIII - The Sea of Sunset

This is the land the sunset washes,
These are the banks of the Yellow
Sea;
Where it rose, or whither it
rushes,

These are the western mystery!

Night after night her purple traffic
Strews the landing with opal
bales;
Merchantmen poise upon
horizons,
Dip, and vanish with fairy sails.

XIV - Purple Clover

There is a flower that bees prefer,
And butterflies desire;
To gain the purple democrat
The humming-birds aspire.

And whatsoever insect pass,
A honey bears away
Proportioned to his several dearth
And her capacity.

Her face is rounder than the moon,
And ruddier than the gown
Of orchis in the pasture,
Or rhododendron worn.

She doth not wait for June;
Before the world is green
Her sturdy little countenance
Against the wind is seen,

Contending with the grass,
Near kinsman to herself,
For privilege of sod and sun,
Sweet litigants for life.

And when the hills are full,
And newer fashions blow,
Doth not retract a single spice
For pang of jealousy.

Her public is the noon,
Her providence the sun,
Her progress by the bee
proclaimed
In sovereign, swerveless tune.

The bravest of the host,
Surrendering the last,
Nor even of defeat aware
When cancelled by the frost.

XV - The Bee

Like trains of cars on tracks of
plush
I hear the level bee:
A jar across the flowers goes,
Their velvet masonry

Withstands until the sweet assault
Their chivalry consumes,
While he, victorious, tilts away
To vanquish other blooms.

His feet are shod with gauze,
His helmet is of gold;
His breast, a single onyx
With chrysoprase, inlaid.

His labor is a chant,
His idleness a tune;
Oh, for a bee's experience
Of clovers and of noon!

XVI.

Presentiment is that long shadow
on the lawn

Indicative that suns go down;
The notice to the startled grass
That darkness is about to pass.

XVII.

As children bid the guest good-
night,
And then reluctant turn,
My flowers raise their pretty lips,
Then put their nightgowns on.

As children caper when they wake,
Merry that it is morn,
My flowers from a hundred cribs
Will peep, and prance again.

XVIII.

Angels in the early morning
May be seen the dews among,
Stooping, plucking, smiling, flying:
Do the buds to them belong?
Angels when the sun is hottest
May be seen the sands among,
Stooping, plucking, sighing, flying;
Parched the flowers they bear
along.

XIX.

So bashful when I spied her,
So pretty, so ashamed!
So hidden in her leaflets,
Lest anybody find;

So breathless till I passed her,
So helpless when I turned
And bore her, struggling, blushing,

Her simple haunts beyond!

For whom I robbed the dingle,
For whom betrayed the dell,
Many will doubtless ask me,
But I shall never tell!

XX - Two Worlds

It makes no difference abroad,
The seasons fit the same,
The mornings blossom into noons,
And split their pods of flame.

Wild-flowers kindle in the woods,
The brooks brag all the day;
No blackbird bates his jargoning
For passing Calvary.

Auto-da-fe and judgment
Are nothing to the bee;
His separation from his rose
To him seems misery.

XXI - The Mountain

The mountain sat upon the plain
In his eternal chair,
His observation omnifold,
His inquest everywhere.

The seasons prayed around his
knees,
Like children round a sire:
Grandfather of the days is he,
Of dawn the ancestor.

XXII - A Day

I'll tell you how the sun rose, —

A ribbon at a time.
The steeples swam in amethyst,
The news like squirrels ran.

The hills untied their bonnets,
The bobolinks begun.
Then I said softly to myself,
"That must have been the sun!"

* * *

But how he set, I know not.
There seemed a purple stile
Which little yellow boys and girls
Were climbing all the while

Till when they reached the other
side,
A dominie in gray
Put gently up the evening bars,
And led the flock away.

XXIII.

The butterfly's assumption-gown,
In chrysoprase apartments hung,
   This afternoon put on.

How condescending to descend,
And be of buttercups the friend
   In a New England town!

XXIV - The Wind

Of all the sounds despatched
abroad,
There's not a charge to me
Like that old measure in the
boughs,

26

That phraseless melody

The wind does, working like a
hand
Whose fingers brush the sky,
Then quiver down, with tufts of
tune
Permitted gods and me.

When winds go round and round
in bands,
And thrum upon the door,
And birds take places overhead,
To bear them orchestra,

I crave him grace, of summer
boughs,
If such an outcast be,
He never heard that fleshless
chant
Rise solemn in the tree,

As if some caravan of sound
On deserts, in the sky,
Had broken rank,
Then knit, and passed
In seamless company.

XXV - Death and Life

Apparently with no surprise
To any happy flower,
The frost beheads it at its play
In accidental power.
The blond assassin passes on,
The sun proceeds unmoved
To measure off another day
For an approving God.

XXVI.

'T was later when the summer
went
Than when the cricket came,
And yet we knew that gentle clock
Meant nought but going home.

'T was sooner when the cricket
went
Than when the winter came,
Yet that pathetic pendulum
Keeps esoteric time.

XXVII - Indian Summer

These are the days when birds
come back,
A very few, a bird or two,
To take a backward look.

These are the days when skies put
on
The old, old sophistries of June, —
A blue and gold mistake.

Oh, fraud that cannot cheat the
bee,
Almost thy plausibility
Induces my belief,

Till ranks of seeds their witness
bear,
And softly through the altered air
Hurries a timid leaf!

Oh, sacrament of summer days,
Oh, last communion in the haze,
Permit a child to join,

Thy sacred emblems to partake,
Thy consecrated bread to break,
Taste thine immortal wine!

XXVIII - Autumn

The morns are meeker than they
were,
The nuts are getting brown;
The berry's cheek is plumper,
The rose is out of town.

The maple wears a gayer scarf,
The field a scarlet gown.
Lest I should be old-fashioned,
I'll put a trinket on.

XXIX - Beclouded

The sky is low, the clouds are
mean,
A travelling flake of snow
Across a barn or through a rut
Debates if it will go.

A narrow wind complains all day
How some one treated him;
Nature, like us, is sometimes
caught
Without her diadem.

XXX - The Hemlock

I think the hemlock likes to stand
Upon a marge of snow;
It suits his own austerity,
And satisfies an awe

That men must slake in
wilderness,
Or in the desert cloy, —
An instinct for the hoar, the bald,
Lapland's necessity.

The hemlock's nature thrives on
cold;
The gnash of northern winds
Is sweetest nutriment to him,
His best Norwegian wines.

To satin races he is nought;
But children on the Don
Beneath his tabernacles play,
And Dnieper wrestlers run.

XXXI.

There's a certain slant of light,
On winter afternoons,
That oppresses, like the weight
Of cathedral tunes.

Heavenly hurt it gives us;
We can find no scar,
But internal difference
Where the meanings are.

None may teach it anything,
' T is the seal, despair, —
An imperial affliction
Sent us of the air.

When it comes, the landscape
listens,
Shadows hold their breath;
When it goes, 't is like the distance
On the look of death.

IV. Time and Eternity

I.

One dignity delays for all,
One mitred afternoon.
None can avoid this purple,
None evade this crown.

Coach it insures, and footmen,
Chamber and state and throng;
Bells, also, in the village,
As we ride grand along.

What dignified attendants,
What service when we pause!
How loyally at parting
Their hundred hats they raise!

How pomp surpassing ermine,
When simple you and I
Present our meek escutcheon,
And claim the rank to die!

II - Too Late

Delayed till she had ceased to know,
Delayed till in its vest of snow
   Her loving bosom lay.
An hour behind the fleeting breath,
Later by just an hour than death,
—
   Oh, lagging yesterday!

Could she have guessed that it would be;
Could but a crier of the glee
   Have climbed the distant hill;
Had not the bliss so slow a pace,
—
Who knows but this surrendered face
   Were undefeated still?

Oh, if there may departing be
Any forgot by victory
   In her imperial round,
Show them this meek apparelled thing,
That could not stop to be a king,
   Doubtful if it be crowned!

III - Astra Castra

Departed to the judgment,
A mighty afternoon;
Great clouds like ushers leaning,
Creation looking on.

The flesh surrendered, cancelled,
The bodiless begun;
Two worlds, like audiences, disperse
And leave the soul alone.

IV.

Safe in their alabaster chambers,
Untouched by morning and untouched by noon,
Sleep the meek members of the resurrection,
Rafter of satin, and roof of stone.

Light laughs the breeze in her
castle of sunshine;
Babbles the bee in a stolid ear;
Pipe the sweet birds in ignorant
cadence, —
Ah, what sagacity perished here!
Grand go the years in the crescent
above them;
Worlds scoop their arcs, and
firmaments row,
Diadems drop and Doges
surrender,
Soundless as dots on a disk of
snow.

V.

On this long storm the rainbow
rose,
On this late morn the sun;
The clouds, like listless elephants,
Horizons straggled down.

The birds rose smiling in their
nests,
The gales indeed were done;
Alas! how heedless were the eyes
On whom the summer shone!

The quiet nonchalance of death
No daybreak can bestir;
The slow archangel's syllables
Must awaken her.

VI - From The Chrysalis

My cocoon tightens, colors tease,
I'm feeling for the air;
A dim capacity for wings

Degrades the dress I wear.

A power of butterfly must be
The aptitude to fly,
Meadows of majesty concedes
And easy sweeps of sky.

So I must baffle at the hint
And cipher at the sign,
And make much blunder, if at last
I take the clew divine.

VII - Setting Sail

Exultation is the going
Of an inland soul to sea, —
Past the houses, past the
headlands,
Into deep eternity!

Bred as we, among the mountains,
Can the sailor understand
The divine intoxication
Of the first league out from land?

VIII.

Look back on time with kindly
eyes,
He doubtless did his best;
How softly sinks his trembling sun
In human nature's west!

IX.

A train went through a burial gate,
A bird broke forth and sang,
And trilled, and quivered, and
shook his throat

Till all the churchyard rang;

And then adjusted his little notes,
And bowed and sang again.
Doubtless, he thought it meet of
him
To say good-by to men.

X.

I died for beauty, but was scarce
Adjusted in the tomb,
When one who died for truth was
lain
In an adjoining room.

He questioned softly why I failed?
"For beauty," I replied.
"And I for truth, — the two are
one;
We brethren are," he said.

And so, as kinsmen met a night,
We talked between the rooms,
Until the moss had reached our
lips,
And covered up our names.

XI - "Troubled About Many Things."

How many times these low feet
staggered,
Only the soldered mouth can tell;
Try! can you stir the awful rivet?
Try! can you lift the hasps of steel?

Stroke the cool forehead, hot so
often,

Lift, if you can, the listless hair;
Handle the adamantine fingers
Never a thimble more shall wear.

Buzz the dull flies on the chamber
window;
Brave shines the sun through the
freckled pane;
Fearless the cobweb swings from
the ceiling —
Indolent housewife, in daisies lain!

XII - Real

I like a look of agony,
Because I know it 's true;
Men do not sham convulsion,
Nor simulate a throe.

The eyes glaze once, and that is
death.
Impossible to feign
The beads upon the forehead
By homely anguish strung.

XIII - The Funeral

That short, potential stir
That each can make but once,
That bustle so illustrious
'T is almost consequence,

Is the eclat of death.
Oh, thou unknown renown
That not a beggar would accept,
Had he the power to spurn!

XIV.

I went to thank her,
But she slept;
Her bed a funnelled stone,
With nosegays at the head and
foot,
That travellers had thrown,

Who went to thank her;
But she slept.
'T was short to cross the sea
To look upon her like, alive,
But turning back 't was slow.

XV.

I've seen a dying eye
Run round and round a room
In search of something, as it
seemed,
Then cloudier become;
And then, obscure with fog,
And then be soldered down,
Without disclosing what it be,
'T were blessed to have seen.

XVI - Refuge

The clouds their backs together
laid,
The north begun to push,
The forests galloped till they fell,
The lightning skipped like mice;
The thunder crumbled like a stuff
—

How good to be safe in tombs,
Where nature's temper cannot
reach,

Nor vengeance ever comes!

XVII.

I never saw a moor,
I never saw the sea;
Yet know I how the heather looks,
And what a wave must be.

I never spoke with God,
Nor visited in heaven;
Yet certain am I of the spot
As if the chart were given.

XVIII - Playmates

God permits industrious angels
Afternoons to play.
I met one, — forgot my school-
mates,
All, for him, straightway.

God calls home the angels
promptly
At the setting sun;
I missed mine. How dreary
marbles,
After playing Crown!

XIX.

To know just how he suffered
would be dear;
To know if any human eyes were
near
To whom he could intrust his
wavering gaze,
Until it settled firm on Paradise.

To know if he was patient, part
content,
Was dying as he thought, or
different;
Was it a pleasant day to die,
And did the sunshine face his way?

What was his furthest mind, of
home, or God,
Or what the distant say
At news that he ceased human
nature
On such a day?

And wishes, had he any?
Just his sigh, accented,
Had been legible to me.
And was he confident until
Ill fluttered out in everlasting
well?

And if he spoke, what name was
best,
What first,
What one broke off with
At the drowsiest?

Was he afraid, or tranquil?
Might he know
How conscious consciousness
could grow,
Till love that was, and love too
blest to be,
Meet — and the junction be
Eternity?

XX.

The last night that she lived,
It was a common night,

Except the dying; this to us
Made nature different.

We noticed smallest things, —
Things overlooked before,
By this great light upon our minds
Italicized, as 't were.

That others could exist
While she must finish quite,
A jealousy for her arose
So nearly infinite.

We waited while she passed;
It was a narrow time,
Too jostled were our souls to
speak,
At length the notice came.

She mentioned, and forgot;
Then lightly as a reed
Bent to the water, shivered scarce,
Consented, and was dead.

And we, we placed the hair,
And drew the head erect;
And then an awful leisure was,
Our faith to regulate.

XXI - The First Lesson

Not in this world to see his face
Sounds long, until I read the place
Where this is said to be
But just the primer to a life
Unopened, rare, upon the shelf,
Clasped yet to him and me.

And yet, my primer suits me so
I would not choose a book to know

Than that, be sweeter wise;
Might some one else so learned be,
And leave me just my A B C,
Himself could have the skies.

XXII.

The bustle in a house
The morning after death
Is solemnest of industries
Enacted upon earth, —

The sweeping up the heart,
And putting love away
We shall not want to use again
Until eternity.

XXIII.

I reason, earth is short,
And anguish absolute,
And many hurt;
But what of that?

I reason, we could die:
The best vitality
Cannot excel decay;
But what of that?

I reason that in heaven
Somehow, it will be even,
Some new equation given;
But what of that?

XXIV.

Afraid? Of whom am I afraid?
Not death; for who is he?
The porter of my father's lodge

As much abasheth me.

Of life? 'T were odd I fear a thing
That comprehendeth me
In one or more existences
At Deity's decree.

Of resurrection? Is the east
Afraid to trust the morn
With her fastidious forehead?
As soon impeach my crown!

XXV - Dying

The sun kept setting, setting still;
No hue of afternoon
Upon the village I perceived, —
From house to house 't was noon.
The dusk kept dropping, dropping still;
No dew upon the grass,
But only on my forehead stopped,
And wandered in my face.

My feet kept drowsing, drowsing still,
My fingers were awake;
Yet why so little sound myself
Unto my seeming make?

How well I knew the light before!
I could not see it now.
'T is dying, I am doing; but
I'm not afraid to know.
XXVI.

Two swimmers wrestled on the spar
Until the morning sun,

When one turned smiling to the
land.
O God, the other one!

The stray ships passing spied a
face
Upon the waters borne,
With eyes in death still begging
raised,
And hands beseeching thrown.

XXVII - The Chariot

Because I could not stop for Death,
He kindly stopped for me;
The carriage held but just
ourselves
And Immortality.

We slowly drove, he knew no
haste,
And I had put away
My labor, and my leisure too,
For his civility.

We passed the school where
children played,
Their lessons scarcely done;
We passed the fields of gazing
grain,
We passed the setting sun.

We paused before a house that
seemed
A swelling of the ground;
The roof was scarcely visible,
The cornice but a mound.

Since then 't is centuries; but each
Feels shorter than the day

I first surmised the horses' heads
Were toward eternity.

XXVIII.

She went as quiet as the dew
From a familiar flower.
Not like the dew did she return
At the accustomed hour!

She dropt as softly as a star
From out my summer's eve;
Less skilful than Leverrier
It's sorer to believe!

XXIX - Resurgam

At last to be identified!
At last, the lamps upon thy side,
The rest of life to see!
Past midnight, past the morning
star!
Past sunrise! Ah! what leagues
there are
Between our feet and day!

XXX.

Except to heaven, she is nought;
Except for angels, lone;
Except to some wide-wandering
bee,
A flower superfluous blown;

Except for winds, provincial;
Except by butterflies,
Unnoticed as a single dew
That on the acre lies.

The smallest housewife in the grass,
Yet take her from the lawn,
And somebody has lost the face
That made existence home!

XXXI.

Death is a dialogue between
The spirit and the dust.
"Dissolve," says Death. The Spirit,
"Sir,
I have another trust."

Death doubts it, argues from the ground.
The Spirit turns away,
Just laying off, for evidence,
An overcoat of clay.

XXXII.

It was too late for man,
But early yet for God;
Creation impotent to help,
But prayer remained our side.

How excellent the heaven,
When earth cannot be had;
How hospitable, then, the face
Of our old neighbor, God!

XXXIII - Along The Potomac

When I was small, a woman died.
To-day her only boy
Went up from the Potomac,
His face all victory,

To look at her; how slowly
The seasons must have turned
Till bullets clipt an angle,
And he passed quickly round!

If pride shall be in Paradise
I never can decide;
Of their imperial conduct,
No person testified.

But proud in apparition,
That woman and her boy
Pass back and forth before my brain,
As ever in the sky.

XXXIV.

The daisy follows soft the sun,
And when his golden walk is done,
    Sits shyly at his feet.
He, waking, finds the flower near.
"Wherefore, marauder, art thou here?"
    "Because, sir, love is sweet!"

We are the flower, Thou the sun!
Forgive us, if as days decline,
    We nearer steal to Thee, —
Enamoured of the parting west,
The peace, the flight, the amethyst,
    Night's possibility!

XXXV - Emancipation

No rack can torture me,
My soul's at liberty
Behind this mortal bone
There knits a bolder one

36

You cannot prick with saw,
Nor rend with scymitar.
Two bodies therefore be;
Bind one, and one will flee.

The eagle of his nest
No easier divest
And gain the sky,
Than mayest thou,

Except thyself may be
Thine enemy;
Captivity is consciousness,
So's liberty.

XXXVI - Lost

I lost a world the other day.
Has anybody found?
You'll know it by the row of stars
Around its forehead bound.
A rich man might not notice it;
Yet to my frugal eye
Of more esteem than ducats.
Oh, find it, sir, for me!

XXXVII.

If I shouldn't be alive
When the robins come,
Give the one in red cravat
A memorial crumb.

If I couldn't thank you,
Being just asleep,
You will know I'm trying
With my granite lip!

XXXVIII.

Sleep is supposed to be,
By souls of sanity,
The shutting of the eye.

Sleep is the station grand
Down which on either hand
The hosts of witness stand!

Morn is supposed to be,
By people of degree,
The breaking of the day.

Morning has not occurred!
That shall aurora be
East of eternity;

One with the banner gay,
One in the red array, —
That is the break of day.

XXXIX.

I shall know why, when time is
over,
And I have ceased to wonder why;
Christ will explain each separate
anguish
In the fair schoolroom of the sky.

He will tell me what Peter
promised,
And I, for wonder at his woe,
I shall forget the drop of anguish
That scalds me now, that scalds
me now.

XL.

I never lost as much but twice,
And that was in the sod;
Twice have I stood a beggar
Before the door of God!

Angels, twice descending,
Reimbursed my store.
Burglar, banker, father,
I am poor once more!

Poems by Emily Dickinson - Second Series

Edited by two of her friends

Mabel Loomis Todd and T.W. Higginson

Preface

The eagerness with which the first volume of Emily Dickinson's poems has been read shows very clearly that all our alleged modern artificiality does not prevent a prompt appreciation of the qualities of directness and simplicity in approaching the greatest themes,—life and love and death. That "irresistible needle-touch," as one of her best critics has called it, piercing at once the very core of a thought, has found a response as wide and sympathetic as it has been unexpected even to those who knew best her compelling power. This second volume, while open to the same criticism as to form with its predecessor, shows also the same shining beauties.

Although Emily Dickinson had been in the habit of sending occasional poems to friends and correspondents, the full extent of her writing was by no means imagined by them. Her friend "H.H." must at least have suspected it, for in a letter dated 5th September, 1884, she wrote:—

My Dear Friend,— What portfolios full of verses you must have! It is a cruel wrong to your "day and generation" that you will not give them light.
If such a thing should happen as that I should outlive you, I wish you would make me your literary legatee and executor. Surely after you are what is called "dead" you will be willing that the poor ghosts you have left behind should be cheered and pleased by your verses, will you not? You ought to be. I do not think we have a right to withhold from the world a word or a thought any more than a deed which might help a single soul. . . .

Truly yours,
  Helen Jackson

The "portfolios" were found, shortly after Emily Dickinson's death, by her sister and only surviving housemate. Most of the poems had been carefully copied on sheets of note-paper, and tied in little fascicules, each of six or eight sheets. While many of them bear evidence of having been thrown off at white heat, still more had received thoughtful revision. There is the frequent addition of rather perplexing foot-notes, affording large choice of words and phrases. And in the copies which she sent to friends, sometimes one form, sometimes another, is found to have been used. Without important exception, her friends have generously placed at the disposal of the Editors any poems they had received from her; and these have given the obvious advantage of comparison among several renderings of the same verse.

To what further rigorous pruning her verses would have been subjected had she published them herself, we cannot know. They should be regarded in many cases as merely the first strong and suggestive sketches of an artist, intended to be embodied at some time in the finished picture. Emily Dickinson appears to have written her first poems in the winter of 1862. In a letter to one of the present Editors the April following, she says, "I made no verse, but one or two, until this winter."

The handwriting was at first somewhat like the delicate, running Italian hand of our elder gentlewomen; but as she advanced in breadth of thought, it grew bolder and more abrupt, until in her latest years each letter stood distinct and separate from its fellows. In most of her poems, particularly the later ones, everything by way of punctuation was discarded, except numerous dashes; and all important words began with capitals. The effect of a page of her more recent manuscript is exceedingly quaint and strong. The fac-simile given in the present volume is from one of the earlier transition periods. Although there is nowhere a date, the handwriting makes it possible to arrange the poems with general chronologic accuracy.

As a rule, the verses were without titles; but "A Country Burial," "A Thunder-Storm," "The Humming-Bird," and a few others were named by their author, frequently at the end,—sometimes only in the accompanying note, if sent to a friend.

The variation of readings, with the fact that she often wrote in pencil and not always clearly, have at times thrown a good deal of responsibility upon her Editors. But all interference not absolutely inevitable has been avoided. The very roughness of her rendering is part of herself, and not lightly to be touched; for it seems in many cases that she intentionally avoided the smoother and more usual rhymes.

Like impressionist pictures, or Wagner's rugged music, the very absence of conventional form challenges attention. In Emily Dickinson's exacting hands, the especial, intrinsic fitness of a particular order of words might not be sacrificed to anything virtually extrinsic; and her verses all show a strange cadence of inner rhythmical music. Lines are always daringly constructed, and the "thought-rhyme" appears frequently,—appealing, indeed, to an unrecognized sense more elusive than hearing.

Emily Dickinson scrutinized everything with clear-eyed frankness. Every subject was proper ground for legitimate study, even the sombre facts of death and burial, and the unknown life beyond. She touches these themes sometimes lightly, sometimes almost humorously, more often with weird and peculiar power; but she is never by any chance frivolous or trivial. And while, as one critic has said, she may exhibit toward God "an Emersonian self-possession," it was because she looked upon all life with a candor as unprejudiced as it is rare.

She had tried society and the world, and found them lacking. She was not an invalid, and she lived in seclusion from no love-disappointment. Her life was the normal blossoming of a nature introspective to a high degree, whose best thought could not exist in pretence.

Storm, wind, the wild March sky, sunsets and dawns; the birds and bees, butterflies and flowers of her garden, with a few trusted human friends, were sufficient companionship. The coming of the first robin was a jubilee beyond crowning of monarch or birthday of pope; the first red leaf hurrying through "the altered air," an epoch. Immortality was close about her; and while never morbid or melancholy, she lived in its presence.

Mabel Loomis Todd.

Amherst, Massachusetts,

August, 1891.

My nosegays are for captives;
Dim, long-expectant eyes,
Fingers denied the plucking,
Patient till paradise,

To such, if they should whisper
Of morning and the moor,
They bear no other errand,
And I, no other prayer

I. Life

I.

I'm nobody! Who are you?
Are you nobody, too?
Then there 's a pair of us — don't
tell!
They 'd banish us, you know.

How dreary to be somebody!
How public, like a frog
To tell your name the livelong day
To an admiring bog!

II.

I bring an unaccustomed wine
To lips long parching, next to
mine,
And summon them to drink.

Crackling with fever, they essay;
I turn my brimming eyes away,
And come next hour to look.

The hands still hug the tardy glass;
The lips I would have cooled, alas!
Are so superfluous cold,

I would as soon attempt to warm
The bosoms where the frost has
lain
Ages beneath the mould.

Some other thirsty there may be
To whom this would have pointed
me

Had it remained to speak.

And so I always bear the cup
If, haply, mine may be the drop
Some pilgrim thirst to slake, —

If, haply, any say to me,
"Unto the little, unto me,"
When I at last awake.

III.

The nearest dream recedes,
unrealized.
     The heaven we chase
     Like the June bee
     Before the school-boy
     Invites the race;
     Stoops to an easy clover —
Dips — evades — teases —
deploys;
     Then to the royal clouds
     Lifts his light pinnace
     Heedless of the boy
Staring, bewildered, at the
mocking sky.

     Homesick for steadfast honey,
     Ah! the bee flies not
That brews that rare variety.

IV.

We play at paste,
Till qualified for pearl,
Then drop the paste,
And deem ourself a fool.
The shapes, though, were similar,
And our new hands

Learned gem-tactics
Practising sands.

V.

I found the phrase to every
thought
I ever had, but one;
And that defies me, — as a hand
Did try to chalk the sun

To races nurtured in the dark; —
How would your own begin?
Can blaze be done in cochineal,
Or noon in mazarin?

VI - Hope

Hope is the thing with feathers
That perches in the soul,
And sings the tune without the
words,
And never stops at all,

And sweetest in the gale is heard;
And sore must be the storm
That could abash the little bird
That kept so many warm.

I 've heard it in the chillest land,
And on the strangest sea;
Yet, never, in extremity,
It asked a crumb of me.

VII - The White Heat

Dare you see a soul at the white
heat?
    Then crouch within the door.
Red is the fire's common tint;

But when the vivid ore

Has sated flame's conditions,
    Its quivering substance plays
Without a color but the light
    Of unanointed blaze.

Least village boasts its blacksmith,
    Whose anvil's even din
Stands symbol for the finer forge
    That soundless tugs within,

Refining these impatient ores
    With hammer and with blaze,
Until the designated light
    Repudiate the forge.

VIII - Triumphant

Who never lost, are unprepared
A coronet to find;
Who never thirsted, flagons
And cooling tamarind.

Who never climbed the weary
league —
Can such a foot explore
The purple territories
On Pizarro's shore?

How many legions overcome?
The emperor will say.
How many colors taken
On Revolution Day?

How many bullets bearest?
The royal scar hast thou?
Angels, write "Promoted"
On this soldier's brow!

IX - The Test

I can wade grief,
Whole pools of it, —
I 'm used to that.
But the least push of joy
Breaks up my feet,
And I tip — drunken.
Let no pebble smile,
'T was the new liquor, —
That was all!

Power is only pain,
Stranded, through discipline,
Till weights will hang.
Give balm to giants,
And they 'll wilt, like men.
Give Himmaleh, —
They 'll carry him!

X - Escape

I never hear the word "escape"
Without a quicker blood,
A sudden expectation,
A flying attitude.

I never hear of prisons broad
By soldiers battered down,
But I tug childish at my bars, —
Only to fail again!

XI - Compensation

For each ecstatic instant
We must an anguish pay
In keen and quivering ratio
To the ecstasy.

For each beloved hour
Sharp pittances of years,
Bitter contested farthings
And coffers heaped with tears.

XII - The Martyrs

Through the straight pass of
suffering
The martyrs even trod,
Their feet upon temptation,
Their faces upon God.

A stately, shriven company;
Convulsion playing round,
Harmless as streaks of meteor
Upon a planet's bound.

Their faith the everlasting troth;
Their expectation fair;
The needle to the north degree
Wades so, through polar air.

XIII - A Prayer

I meant to have but modest needs,
Such as content, and heaven;
Within my income these could lie,
And life and I keep even.

But since the last included both,
It would suffice my prayer
But just for one to stipulate,
And grace would grant the pair.

And so, upon this wise I prayed, —
Great Spirit, give to me
A heaven not so large as yours,
But large enough for me.

A smile suffused Jehovah's face;
The cherubim withdrew;
Grave saints stole out to look at
me,
And showed their dimples, too.

I left the place with all my might,
—
My prayer away I threw;
The quiet ages picked it up,
And Judgment twinkled, too,

That one so honest be extant
As take the tale for true
That "Whatsoever you shall ask,
Itself be given you."

But I, grown shrewder, scan the
skies
With a suspicious air, —
As children, swindled for the first,
All swindlers be, infer.

XIV.

The thought beneath so slight a
film
Is more distinctly seen, —
As laces just reveal the surge,
Or mists the Apennine.

XV.

The soul unto itself
Is an imperial friend, —
Or the most agonizing spy
An enemy could send.

Secure against its own,

No treason it can fear;
Itself its sovereign, of itself
The soul should stand in awe.

XVI.

Surgeons must be very careful
When they take the knife!
Underneath their fine incisions
Stirs the culprit, — Life!

XVII - The Railway Train

I like to see it lap the miles,
And lick the valleys up,
And stop to feed itself at tanks;
And then, prodigious, step

Around a pile of mountains,
And, supercilious, peer
In shanties by the sides of roads;
And then a quarry pare

To fit its sides, and crawl between,
Complaining all the while
In horrid, hooting stanza;
Then chase itself down hill

And neigh like Boanerges;
Then, punctual as a star,
Stop — docile and omnipotent —
At its own stable door.

XVIII - The Show

The show is not the show,
But they that go.
Menagerie to me
My neighbor be.

Fair play —
Both went to see.

XIX.

Delight becomes pictorial
When viewed through pain, —
More fair, because impossible
That any gain.
The mountain at a given distance
In amber lies;
Approached, the amber flits a
little, —
And that 's the skies!

XX.

A thought went up my mind to-
day
That I have had before,
But did not finish, — some way
back,
I could not fix the year,

Nor where it went, nor why it
came
The second time to me,
Nor definitely what it was,
Have I the art to say.

But somewhere in my soul, I know
I 've met the thing before;
It just reminded me — 't was all —
And came my way no more.

XXI.

Is Heaven a physician?
They say that He can heal;

But medicine posthumous
Is unavailable.

Is Heaven an exchequer?
They speak of what we owe;
But that negotiation
I 'm not a party to.

XXII - The Return

Though I get home how late, how
late!
So I get home, 't will compensate.
Better will be the ecstasy
That they have done expecting me,
When, night descending, dumb
and dark,
They hear my unexpected knock.
Transporting must the moment
be,
Brewed from decades of agony!

To think just how the fire will
burn,
Just how long-cheated eyes will
turn
To wonder what myself will say,
And what itself will say to me,
Beguiles the centuries of way!

XXIII.

A poor torn heart, a tattered heart,
That sat it down to rest,
Nor noticed that the ebbing day
Flowed silver to the west,
Nor noticed night did soft descend
Nor constellation burn,
Intent upon the vision

Of latitudes unknown.

The angels, happening that way,
This dusty heart espied;
Tenderly took it up from toil
And carried it to God.
There, — sandals for the barefoot;
There, — gathered from the gales,
Do the blue havens by the hand
Lead the wandering sails.

XXIV - Too Much

I should have been too glad, I see,
Too lifted for the scant degree
    Of life's penurious round;
My little circuit would have
shamed
This new circumference, have
blamed
    The homelier time behind.

I should have been too saved, I
see,
Too rescued; fear too dim to me
    That I could spell the prayer
I knew so perfect yesterday, —
That scalding one, "Sabachthani,"
    Recited fluent here.

Earth would have been too much, I
see,
And heaven not enough for me;
    I should have had the joy
Without the fear to justify, —
The palm without the Calvary;
    So, Saviour, crucify.

Defeat whets victory, they say;
The reefs in old Gethsemane

Endear the shore beyond.
'T is beggars banquets best define;
'T is thirsting vitalizes wine, —
    Faith faints to understand.

XXV - Shipwreck

It tossed and tossed, —
A little brig I knew, —
O'ertook by blast,
It spun and spun,
And groped delirious, for morn.

It slipped and slipped,
As one that drunken stepped;
Its white foot tripped,
Then dropped from sight.

Ah, brig, good-night
To crew and you;
The ocean's heart too smooth, too
blue,
To break for you.

XXVI.

Victory comes late,
And is held low to freezing lips
Too rapt with frost
To take it.
How sweet it would have tasted,
Just a drop!
Was God so economical?
His table 's spread too high for us
Unless we dine on tip-toe.
Crumbs fit such little mouths,
Cherries suit robins;
The eagle's golden breakfast
Strangles them.

God keeps his oath to sparrows,
Who of little love
Know how to starve!

XXVII - Enough

God gave a loaf to every bird,
But just a crumb to me;
I dare not eat it, though I starve, —
My poignant luxury
To own it, touch it, prove the feat
That made the pellet mine, —
Too happy in my sparrow chance
For ampler coveting.

It might be famine all around,
I could not miss an ear,
Such plenty smiles upon my
board,
My garner shows so fair.
I wonder how the rich may feel, —
An Indiaman — an Earl?
I deem that I with but a crumb
Am sovereign of them all.

XXVIII.

Experiment to me
Is every one I meet.
If it contain a kernel?
The figure of a nut

Presents upon a tree,
Equally plausibly;
But meat within is requisite,
To squirrels and to me.

XXIX - My Country's Wardrobe

My country need not change her
gown,
Her triple suit as sweet
As when 't was cut at Lexington,
And first pronounced "a fit."

Great Britain disapproves "the
stars;"
Disparagement discreet, —
There 's something in their
attitude
That taunts her bayonet.

XXX.

Faith is a fine invention
For gentlemen who see;
But microscopes are prudent
In an emergency!

XXXI.

Except the heaven had come so
near,
So seemed to choose my door,
The distance would not haunt me
so;
I had not hoped before.

But just to hear the grace depart
I never thought to see,
Afflicts me with a double loss;
'T is lost, and lost to me.

XXXII.

Portraits are to daily faces
As an evening west
To a fine, pedantic sunshine
In a satin vest.

XXXIII - The Duel

I took my power in my hand.
And went against the world;
'T was not so much as David had,
But I was twice as bold.

I aimed my pebble, but myself
Was all the one that fell.
Was it Goliath was too large,
Or only I too small?

XXXIV.

A shady friend for torrid days
Is easier to find
Than one of higher temperature
For frigid hour of mind.

The vane a little to the east
Scares muslin souls away;
If broadcloth breasts are firmer
Than those of organdy,

Who is to blame? The weaver?
Ah! the bewildering thread!
The tapestries of paradise
So notelessly are made!

XXXV - The Goal

Each life converges to some centre
Expressed or still;
Exists in every human nature
A goal,

Admitted scarcely to itself, it may
be,
Too fair
For credibility's temerity
To dare.

Adored with caution, as a brittle
heaven,
To reach
Were hopeless as the rainbow's
raiment
To touch,

Yet persevered toward, surer for
the distance;
How high
Unto the saints' slow diligence
The sky!

Ungained, it may be, by a life's low
venture,
But then,
Eternity enables the endeavoring
Again.

XXXVI - Sight

Before I got my eye put out,
I liked as well to see
As other creatures that have eyes,
And know no other way.

But were it told to me, to-day,

That I might have the sky
For mine, I tell you that my heart
Would split, for size of me.

The meadows mine, the
mountains mine, —
All forests, stintless stars,
As much of noon as I could take
Between my finite eyes.

The motions of the dipping birds,
The lightning's jointed road,
For mine to look at when I liked,
—
The news would strike me dead!

So safer, guess, with just my soul
Upon the window-pane
Where other creatures put their
eyes,
Incautious of the sun.

XXXVII.

Talk with prudence to a beggar
Of 'Potosi' and the mines!
Reverently to the hungry
Of your viands and your wines!

Cautious, hint to any captive
You have passed enfranchised
feet!
Anecdotes of air in dungeons
Have sometimes proved deadly
sweet!

XXXVIII - The Preacher

He preached upon "breadth" till it
argued him narrow, —
The broad are too broad to define;
And of "truth" until it proclaimed
him a liar, —
The truth never flaunted a sign.

Simplicity fled from his counterfeit
presence
As gold the pyrites would shun.
What confusion would cover the
innocent Jesus
To meet so enabled a man!

XXXIX.

Good night! which put the candle
out?
A jealous zephyr, not a doubt.
    Ah! friend, you little knew
How long at that celestial wick
The angels labored diligent;
    Extinguished, now, for you!

It might have been the lighthouse
spark
Some sailor, rowing in the dark,
    Had importuned to see!
It might have been the waning
lamp
That lit the drummer from the
camp
    To purer reveille!

XL.

When I hoped I feared,

Since I hoped I dared;
Everywhere alone
As a church remain;
Spectre cannot harm,
Serpent cannot charm;
He deposes doom,
Who hath suffered him.

XLI - Deed

A deed knocks first at thought,
And then it knocks at will.
That is the manufacturing spot,
And will at home and well.

It then goes out an act,
Or is entombed so still
That only to the ear of God
Its doom is audible.

XLII - Time's Lesson

Mine enemy is growing old, —
I have at last revenge.
The palate of the hate departs;
If any would avenge, —

Let him be quick, the viand flits,
It is a faded meat.
Anger as soon as fed is dead;
'T is starving makes it fat.

XLIII - Remorse

Remorse is memory awake,
Her companies astir, —
A presence of departed acts
At window and at door.

It's past set down before the soul,
And lighted with a match,
Perusal to facilitate
Of its condensed despatch.

Remorse is cureless, — the disease
Not even God can heal;
For 't is his institution, —
The complement of hell.

XLIV - The Shelter

The body grows outside, —
The more convenient way, —
That if the spirit like to hide,
Its temple stands alway

Ajar, secure, inviting;
It never did betray
The soul that asked its shelter
In timid honesty.

XLV.

Undue significance a starving man attaches
To food
Far off; he sighs, and therefore hopeless,
And therefore good.

Partaken, it relieves indeed, but proves us
That spices fly
In the receipt. It was the distance
Was savory.

XLVI.

Heart not so heavy as mine,
Wending late home,
As it passed my window
Whistled itself a tune, —

A careless snatch, a ballad,
A ditty of the street;
Yet to my irritated ear
An anodyne so sweet,

It was as if a bobolink,
Sauntering this way,
Carolled and mused and carolled,
Then bubbled slow away.

It was as if a chirping brook
Upon a toilsome way
Set bleeding feet to minuets
Without the knowing why.

To-morrow, night will come again,
Weary, perhaps, and sore.
Ah, bugle, by my window,
I pray you stroll once more!

XLVII.

I many times thought peace had
come,
When peace was far away;
As wrecked men deem they sight
the land
At centre of the sea,

And struggle slacker, but to prove,
As hopelessly as I,
How many the fictitious shores
Before the harbor lie.

XLVIII.

Unto my books so good to turn
Far ends of tired days;
It half endears the abstinence,
And pain is missed in praise.

As flavors cheer retarded guests
With banquetings to be,
So spices stimulate the time
Till my small library.

It may be wilderness without,
Far feet of failing men,
But holiday excludes the night,
And it is bells within.

I thank these kinsmen of the shelf;
Their countenances bland
Enamour in prospective,
And satisfy, obtained.

XLIX.

This merit hath the worst, —
It cannot be again.
When Fate hath taunted last
And thrown her furthest stone,

The maimed may pause and
breathe,
And glance securely round.
The deer invites no longer
Than it eludes the hound.

L - Hunger

I had been hungry all the years;
My noon had come, to dine;

I, trembling, drew the table near,
And touched the curious wine.

'T was this on tables I had seen,
When turning, hungry, lone,
I looked in windows, for the
wealth
I could not hope to own.

I did not know the ample bread,
'T was so unlike the crumb
The birds and I had often shared
In Nature's dining-room.

The plenty hurt me, 't was so new,
—
Myself felt ill and odd,
As berry of a mountain bush
Transplanted to the road.

Nor was I hungry; so I found
That hunger was a way
Of persons outside windows,
The entering takes away.

LI.

I gained it so,
    By climbing slow,
By catching at the twigs that grow
Between the bliss and me.
    It hung so high,
    As well the sky
    Attempt by strategy.

I said I gained it, —
    This was all.
Look, how I clutch it,
    Lest it fall,
And I a pauper go;

Unfitted by an instant's grace
For the contented beggar's face
I wore an hour ago.

LII.

To learn the transport by the pain,
As blind men learn the sun;
To die of thirst, suspecting
That brooks in meadows run;

To stay the homesick, homesick
feet
Upon a foreign shore
Haunted by native lands, the
while,
And blue, beloved air —

This is the sovereign anguish,
This, the signal woe!
These are the patient laureates
Whose voices, trained below,

Ascend in ceaseless carol,
Inaudible, indeed,
To us, the duller scholars
Of the mysterious bard!

LIII - Returning

I years had been from home,
And now, before the door,
I dared not open, lest a face
I never saw before

Stare vacant into mine
And ask my business there.
My business, — just a life I left,
Was such still dwelling there?

I fumbled at my nerve,
I scanned the windows near;
The silence like an ocean rolled,
And broke against my ear.

I laughed a wooden laugh
That I could fear a door,
Who danger and the dead had
faced,
But never quaked before.

I fitted to the latch
My hand, with trembling care,
Lest back the awful door should
spring,
And leave me standing there.

I moved my fingers off
As cautiously as glass,
And held my ears, and like a thief
Fled gasping from the house.

LIV - Prayer

Prayer is the little implement
Through which men reach
Where presence is denied them.
They fling their speech

By means of it in God's ear;
If then He hear,
This sums the apparatus
Comprised in prayer.

LV.

I know that he exists
Somewhere, in silence.

He has hid his rare life
From our gross eyes.

'T is an instant's play,
'T is a fond ambush,
Just to make bliss
Earn her own surprise!

But should the play
Prove piercing earnest,
Should the glee glaze
In death's stiff stare,

Would not the fun
Look too expensive?
Would not the jest
Have crawled too far?

LVI - Melodies Unheard

Musicians wrestle everywhere:
All day, among the crowded air,
    I hear the silver strife;
And — waking long before the
dawn —
Such transport breaks upon the
town
    I think it that "new life!"

It is not bird, it has no nest;
Nor band, in brass and scarlet
dressed,
    Nor tambourine, nor man;
It is not hymn from pulpit read, —
The morning stars the treble led
    On time's first afternoon!

Some say it is the spheres at play!
Some say that bright majority
    Of vanished dames and men!

Some think it service in the place
Where we, with late, celestial face,
    Please God, shall ascertain!

LVII - Called Back

Just lost when I was saved!
Just felt the world go by!
Just girt me for the onset with
eternity,
When breath blew back,
And on the other side
I heard recede the disappointed
tide!

Therefore, as one returned, I feel,
Odd secrets of the line to tell!
Some sailor, skirting foreign
shores,
Some pale reporter from the awful
doors
Before the seal!

Next time, to stay!
Next time, the things to see
By ear unheard,
Unscrutinized by eye.

Next time, to tarry,
While the ages steal, —
Slow tramp the centuries,
And the cycles wheel.

II. Love

I - Choice

Of all the souls that stand create
I have elected one.
When sense from spirit files away,
And subterfuge is done;

When that which is and that which
was
Apart, intrinsic, stand,
And this brief tragedy of flesh
Is shifted like a sand;

When figures show their royal
front
And mists are carved away, —
Behold the atom I preferred
To all the lists of clay!

II.

I have no life but this,
To lead it here;
Nor any death, but lest
Dispelled from there;

Nor tie to earths to come,
Nor action new,
Except through this extent,
The realm of you.

III.

Your riches taught me poverty.
Myself a millionnaire
In little wealths, — as girls could
boast, —
Till broad as Buenos Ayre,

You drifted your dominions
A different Peru;
And I esteemed all poverty,
For life's estate with you.

Of mines I little know, myself,
But just the names of gems, —
The colors of the commonest;
And scarce of diadems

So much that, did I meet the
queen,
Her glory I should know:
But this must be a different
wealth,
To miss it beggars so.

I 'm sure 't is India all day
To those who look on you
Without a stint, without a blame,
—
Might I but be the Jew!

I 'm sure it is Golconda,
Beyond my power to deem, —
To have a smile for mine each day,
How better than a gem!

At least, it solaces to know
That there exists a gold,
Although I prove it just in time
Its distance to behold!

It 's far, far treasure to surmise,
And estimate the pearl
That slipped my simple fingers
through

While just a girl at school!

IV - The Contract

I gave myself to him,
And took himself for pay.
The solemn contract of a life
Was ratified this way.

The wealth might disappoint,
Myself a poorer prove
Than this great purchaser suspect,
The daily own of Love

Depreciate the vision;
But, till the merchant buy,
Still fable, in the isles of spice,
The subtle cargoes lie.

At least, 't is mutual risk, —
Some found it mutual gain;
Sweet debt of Life, — each night to
owe,
Insolvent, every noon.

V - The Letter

"Going to him! Happy letter! Tell
him —
Tell him the page I didn't write;
Tell him I only said the syntax,
And left the verb and the pronoun
out.
Tell him just how the fingers
hurried,
Then how they waded, slow, slow,
slow;
And then you wished you had eyes
in your pages,
So you could see what moved
them so.

"Tell him it wasn't a practised
writer,
You guessed, from the way the
sentence toiled;
You could hear the bodice tug,
behind you,
As if it held but the might of a
child;
You almost pitied it, you, it
worked so.
Tell him — No, you may quibble
there,
For it would split his heart to
know it,
And then you and I were silenter.

"Tell him night finished before we
finished,
And the old clock kept neighing
'day!'
And you got sleepy and begged to
be ended —
What could it hinder so, to say?
Tell him just how she sealed you,
cautious,
But if he ask where you are hid
Until to-morrow, — happy letter!
Gesture, coquette, and shake your
head!"

VI.

The way I read a letter 's this:
'T is first I lock the door,
And push it with my fingers next,
For transport it be sure.

58

And then I go the furthest off
To counteract a knock;
Then draw my little letter forth
And softly pick its lock.

Then, glancing narrow at the wall,
And narrow at the floor,
For firm conviction of a mouse
Not exorcised before,
Peruse how infinite I am
To — no one that you know!
And sigh for lack of heaven, — but not
The heaven the creeds bestow.

VII.

Wild nights! Wild nights!
Were I with thee,
Wild nights should be
Our luxury!

Futile the winds
To a heart in port, —
Done with the compass,
Done with the chart.

Rowing in Eden!
Ah! the sea!
Might I but moor
To-night in thee!

VIII - At Home

The night was wide, and furnished scant
With but a single star,
That often as a cloud it met
Blew out itself for fear.

The wind pursued the little bush,
And drove away the leaves
November left; then clambered up
And fretted in the eaves.

No squirrel went abroad;
A dog's belated feet
Like intermittent plush were heard
Adown the empty street.
To feel if blinds be fast,
And closer to the fire
Her little rocking-chair to draw,
And shiver for the poor,

The housewife's gentle task.
"How pleasanter," said she
Unto the sofa opposite,
"The sleet than May — no thee!"

IX - Possession

Did the harebell loose her girdle
To the lover bee,
Would the bee the harebell hallow
Much as formerly?

Did the paradise, persuaded,
Yield her moat of pearl,
Would the Eden be an Eden,
Or the earl an earl?

X.

A charm invests a face
Imperfectly beheld, —
The lady dare not lift her veil
For fear it be dispelled.

But peers beyond her mesh,
And wishes, and denies, —
Lest interview annul a want
That image satisfies.

XI - The Lovers

The rose did caper on her cheek,
Her bodice rose and fell,
Her pretty speech, like drunken
men,
Did stagger pitiful.

Her fingers fumbled at her work,
—
Her needle would not go;
What ailed so smart a little maid
It puzzled me to know,

Till opposite I spied a cheek
That bore another rose;
Just opposite, another speech
That like the drunkard goes;

A vest that, like the bodice, danced
To the immortal tune, —
Till those two troubled little clocks
Ticked softly into one.

XII.

In lands I never saw, they say,
Immortal Alps look down,
Whose bonnets touch the
firmament,
Whose sandals touch the town, —

Meek at whose everlasting feet
A myriad daisies play.

Which, sir, are you, and which am
I,
Upon an August day?

XIII.

The moon is distant from the sea,
And yet with amber hands
She leads him, docile as a boy,
Along appointed sands.

He never misses a degree;
Obedient to her eye,
He comes just so far toward the
town,
Just so far goes away.

Oh, Signor, thine the amber hand,
And mine the distant sea, —
Obedient to the least command
Thine eyes impose on me.

XIV.

He put the belt around my life, —
I heard the buckle snap,
And turned away, imperial,
My lifetime folding up
Deliberate, as a duke would do
A kingdom's title-deed, —
Henceforth a dedicated sort,
A member of the cloud.

Yet not too far to come at call,
And do the little toils
That make the circuit of the rest,
And deal occasional smiles
To lives that stoop to notice mine
And kindly ask it in, —

Whose invitation, knew you not
For whom I must decline?

XV - The Lost Jewel

I held a jewel in my fingers
And went to sleep.
The day was warm, and winds
were prosy;
I said: "'T will keep."

I woke and chid my honest fingers,
—
The gem was gone;
And now an amethyst
remembrance
Is all I own.

XVI.

What if I say I shall not wait?
What if I burst the fleshly gate
And pass, escaped, to thee?
What if I file this mortal off,
See where it hurt me, — that 's
enough, —
And wade in liberty?

They cannot take us any more, —
Dungeons may call, and guns
implore;
Unmeaning now, to me,
As laughter was an hour ago,
Or laces, or a travelling show,
Or who died yesterday!

III. Nature

I - Mother Nature

Nature, the gentlest mother,
Impatient of no child,
The feeblest or the waywardest,
—
Her admonition mild

In forest and the hill
By traveller is heard,
Restraining rampant squirrel
Or too impetuous bird.

How fair her conversation,
A summer afternoon, —
Her household, her assembly;
And when the sun goes down

Her voice among the aisles
Incites the timid prayer
Of the minutest cricket,
The most unworthy flower.

When all the children sleep
She turns as long away
As will suffice to light her lamps;
Then, bending from the sky

With infinite affection
And infiniter care,
Her golden finger on her lip,
Wills silence everywhere.

II - Out Of The Morning

Will there really be a morning?

Is there such a thing as day?
Could I see it from the mountains
If I were as tall as they?

Has it feet like water-lilies?
Has it feathers like a bird?
Is it brought from famous
countries
Of which I have never heard?

Oh, some scholar! Oh, some sailor!
Oh, some wise man from the skies!
Please to tell a little pilgrim
Where the place called morning
lies!

III.

At half-past three a single bird
Unto a silent sky
Propounded but a single term
Of cautious melody.

At half-past four, experiment
Had subjugated test,
And lo! her silver principle
Supplanted all the rest.

At half-past seven, element
Nor implement was seen,
And place was where the presence
was,
Circumference between.

IV - Day's Parlor

The day came slow, till five
o'clock,
Then sprang before the hills

Like hindered rubies, or the light
A sudden musket spills.

The purple could not keep the
east,
The sunrise shook from fold,
Like breadths of topaz, packed a
night,
The lady just unrolled.

The happy winds their timbrels
took;
The birds, in docile rows,
Arranged themselves around their
prince
(The wind is prince of those).

The orchard sparkled like a Jew,
—
How mighty 't was, to stay
A guest in this stupendous place,
The parlor of the day!

V - The Sun's Wooing

The sun just touched the morning;
The morning, happy thing,
Supposed that he had come to
dwell,
And life would be all spring.

She felt herself supremer, —
A raised, ethereal thing;
Henceforth for her what holiday!
Meanwhile, her wheeling king

Trailed slow along the orchards
His haughty, spangled hems,
Leaving a new necessity, —
The want of diadems!

The morning fluttered, staggered,
Felt feebly for her crown, —
Her unanointed forehead
Henceforth her only one.

VI - The Robin

The robin is the one
That interrupts the morn
With hurried, few, express reports
When March is scarcely on.

The robin is the one
That overflows the noon
With her cherubic quantity,
An April but begun.

The robin is the one
That speechless from her nest
Submits that home and certainty
And sanctity are best.

VII - The Butterfly's Day

From cocoon forth a butterfly
As lady from her door
Emerged — a summer afternoon
—
Repairing everywhere,

Without design, that I could trace,
Except to stray abroad
On miscellaneous enterprise
The clovers understood.

Her pretty parasol was seen
Contracting in a field
Where men made hay, then
struggling hard
With an opposing cloud,

Where parties, phantom as
herself,
To Nowhere seemed to go
In purposeless circumference,
As 't were a tropic show.

And notwithstanding bee that
worked,
And flower that zealous blew,
This audience of idleness
Disdained them, from the sky,

Till sundown crept, a steady tide,
And men that made the hay,
And afternoon, and butterfly,
Extinguished in its sea.

VIII - The Bluebird

Before you thought of spring,
Except as a surmise,
You see, God bless his suddenness,
A fellow in the skies
Of independent hues,
A little weather-worn,
Inspiriting habiliments
Of indigo and brown.

With specimens of song,
As if for you to choose,
Discretion in the interval,
With gay delays he goes
To some superior tree
Without a single leaf,
And shouts for joy to nobody
But his seraphic self!

IX - April

An altered look about the hills;
A Tyrian light the village fills;
A wider sunrise in the dawn;
A deeper twilight on the lawn;
A print of a vermilion foot;
A purple finger on the slope;
A flippant fly upon the pane;
A spider at his trade again;
An added strut in chanticleer;
A flower expected everywhere;
An axe shrill singing in the woods;
Fern-odors on untravelled roads,
—

All this, and more I cannot tell,
A furtive look you know as well,
And Nicodemus' mystery
Receives its annual reply.

X - The Sleeping Flowers

"Whose are the little beds," I
asked,
"Which in the valleys lie?"
Some shook their heads, and
others smiled,
And no one made reply.

"Perhaps they did not hear," I said;
"I will inquire again.
Whose are the beds, the tiny beds
So thick upon the plain?"

"'T is daisy in the shortest;
A little farther on,
Nearest the door to wake the first,
Little leontodon.

"'T is iris, sir, and aster,

Anemone and bell,
Batschia in the blanket red,
And chubby daffodil."

Meanwhile at many cradles
Her busy foot she plied,
Humming the quaintest lullaby
That ever rocked a child.

"Hush! Epigea wakens! —
The crocus stirs her lids,
Rhodora's cheek is crimson, —
She's dreaming of the woods."

Then, turning from them, reverent,
"Their bed-time 't is," she said;
"The bumble-bees will wake them
When April woods are red."

XI - My Rose

Pigmy seraphs gone astray,
Velvet people from Vevay,
Belles from some lost summer day,
Bees' exclusive coterie.
Paris could not lay the fold
Belted down with emerald;
Venice could not show a cheek
Of a tint so lustrous meek.
Never such an ambuscade
As of brier and leaf displayed
For my little damask maid.
I had rather wear her grace
Than an earl's distinguished face;
I had rather dwell like her
Than be Duke of Exeter
Royalty enough for me
To subdue the bumble-bee!

XII - The Oriole's Secret

To hear an oriole sing
May be a common thing,
Or only a divine.

It is not of the bird
Who sings the same, unheard,
As unto crowd.

The fashion of the ear
Attireth that it hear
In dun or fair.
So whether it be rune,
Or whether it be none,
Is of within;

The "tune is in the tree,"
The sceptic showeth me;
"No, sir! In thee!"

XIII - The Oriole

One of the ones that Midas touched,
Who failed to touch us all,
Was that confiding prodigal,
The blissful oriole.

So drunk, he disavows it
With badinage divine;
So dazzling, we mistake him
For an alighting mine.

A pleader, a dissembler,
An epicure, a thief, —
Betimes an oratorio,
An ecstasy in chief;

The Jesuit of orchards,

He cheats as he enchants
Of an entire attar
For his decamping wants.

The splendor of a Burmah,
The meteor of birds,
Departing like a pageant
Of ballads and of bards.

I never thought that Jason sought
For any golden fleece;
But then I am a rural man,
With thoughts that make for
peace.

But if there were a Jason,
Tradition suffer me
Behold his lost emolument
Upon the apple-tree.

XIV - In Shadow

I dreaded that first robin so,
But he is mastered now,
And I 'm accustomed to him
grown, —
He hurts a little, though.

I thought if I could only live
Till that first shout got by,
Not all pianos in the woods
Had power to mangle me.

I dared not meet the daffodils,
For fear their yellow gown
Would pierce me with a fashion
So foreign to my own.

I wished the grass would hurry,
So when 't was time to see,

He 'd be too tall, the tallest one
Could stretch to look at me.

I could not bear the bees should
come,
I wished they 'd stay away
In those dim countries where they
go:
What word had they for me?

They 're here, though; not a
creature failed,
No blossom stayed away
In gentle deference to me,
The Queen of Calvary.

Each one salutes me as he goes,
And I my childish plumes
Lift, in bereaved acknowledgment
Of their unthinking drums.

XV - The Humming-Bird

A route of evanescence
With a revolving wheel;
A resonance of emerald,
A rush of cochineal;
And every blossom on the bush
Adjusts its tumbled head, —
The mail from Tunis, probably,
An easy morning's ride.

XVI - Secrets

The skies can't keep their secret!
They tell it to the hills —
The hills just tell the orchards —
And they the daffodils!

A bird, by chance, that goes that
way

Soft overheard the whole.
If I should bribe the little bird,
Who knows but she would tell?

I think I won't, however,
It's finer not to know;
If summer were an axiom,
What sorcery had snow?

So keep your secret, Father!
I would not, if I could,
Know what the sapphire fellows
do,
In your new-fashioned world!

XVII.

Who robbed the woods,
The trusting woods?
The unsuspecting trees
Brought out their burrs and
mosses
His fantasy to please.
He scanned their trinkets, curious,
He grasped, he bore away.
What will the solemn hemlock,
What will the fir-tree say?

XVIII - Two Voyagers

Two butterflies went out at noon
And waltzed above a stream,
Then stepped straight through the
firmament
And rested on a beam;

And then together bore away
Upon a shining sea, —
Though never yet, in any port,

Their coming mentioned be.

If spoken by the distant bird,
If met in ether sea
By frigate or by merchantman,
Report was not to me.

XIX - By The Sea

I started early, took my dog,
And visited the sea;
The mermaids in the basement
Came out to look at me,

And frigates in the upper floor
Extended hempen hands,
Presuming me to be a mouse
Aground, upon the sands.

But no man moved me till the tide
Went past my simple shoe,
And past my apron and my belt,
And past my bodice too,

And made as he would eat me up
As wholly as a dew
Upon a dandelion's sleeve —
And then I started too.

And he — he followed close
behind;
I felt his silver heel
Upon my ankle, — then my shoes
Would overflow with pearl.

Until we met the solid town,
No man he seemed to know;
And bowing with a mighty look
At me, the sea withdrew.

XX - Old-Fashioned

Arcturus is his other name, —
I'd rather call him star!
It's so unkind of science
To go and interfere!

I pull a flower from the woods, —
A monster with a glass
Computes the stamens in a breath,
And has her in a class.

Whereas I took the butterfly
Aforetime in my hat,
He sits erect in cabinets,
The clover-bells forgot.

What once was heaven, is zenith
now.
Where I proposed to go
When time's brief masquerade
was done,
Is mapped, and charted too!

What if the poles should frisk
about
And stand upon their heads!
I hope I 'm ready for the worst,
Whatever prank betides!

Perhaps the kingdom of Heaven 's
changed!
I hope the children there
Won't be new-fashioned when I
come,
And laugh at me, and stare!

I hope the father in the skies
Will lift his little girl, —
Old-fashioned, naughty,
everything, —

Over the stile of pearl!

XXI - A Tempest

An awful tempest mashed the air,
The clouds were gaunt and few;
A black, as of a spectre's cloak,
Hid heaven and earth from view.

The creatures chuckled on the
roofs
And whistled in the air,
And shook their fists and gnashed
their teeth.
And swung their frenzied hair.

The morning lit, the birds arose;
The monster's faded eyes
Turned slowly to his native coast,
And peace was Paradise!

XXII - The Sea.

An everywhere of silver,
With ropes of sand
To keep it from effacing
The track called land.

XXIII - In The Garden

A bird came down the walk:
He did not know I saw;
He bit an angle-worm in halves
And ate the fellow, raw.

And then he drank a dew
From a convenient grass,
And then hopped sidewise to the
wall

To let a beetle pass.

He glanced with rapid eyes
That hurried all abroad, —
They looked like frightened beads,
I thought;
He stirred his velvet head

Like one in danger; cautious,
I offered him a crumb,
And he unrolled his feathers
And rowed him softer home

Than oars divide the ocean,
Too silver for a seam,
Or butterflies, off banks of noon,
Leap, plashless, as they swim.

XXIV - The Snake

A narrow fellow in the grass
Occasionally rides;
You may have met him, — did you
not,
His notice sudden is.

The grass divides as with a comb,
A spotted shaft is seen;
And then it closes at your feet
And opens further on.

He likes a boggy acre,
A floor too cool for corn.
Yet when a child, and barefoot,
I more than once, at morn,

Have passed, I thought, a whip-
lash
Unbraiding in the sun, —
When, stooping to secure it,

It wrinkled, and was gone.

Several of nature's people
I know, and they know me;
I feel for them a transport
Of cordiality;

But never met this fellow,
Attended or alone,
Without a tighter breathing,
And zero at the bone.

XXV - The Mushroom

The mushroom is the elf of plants,
At evening it is not;
At morning in a truffled hut
It stops upon a spot

As if it tarried always;
And yet its whole career
Is shorter than a snake's delay,
And fleeter than a tare.

'T is vegetation's juggler,
The germ of alibi;
Doth like a bubble antedate,
And like a bubble hie.

I feel as if the grass were pleased
To have it intermit;
The surreptitious scion
Of summer's circumspect.

Had nature any outcast face,
Could she a son contemn,
Had nature an Iscariot,
That mushroom, — it is him.

XXVI - The Storm

There came a wind like a bugle;
It quivered through the grass,
And a green chill upon the heat
So ominous did pass
We barred the windows and the
doors
As from an emerald ghost;
The doom's electric moccason
That very instant passed.
On a strange mob of panting trees,
And fences fled away,
And rivers where the houses ran
The living looked that day.
The bell within the steeple wild
The flying tidings whirled.
How much can come
And much can go,
And yet abide the world!

XXVII - The Spider

A spider sewed at night
Without a light
Upon an arc of white.
If ruff it was of dame
Or shroud of gnome,
Himself, himself inform.
Of immortality
His strategy
Was physiognomy.

XXVIII.

I know a place where summer
strives
With such a practised frost,
She each year leads her daisies
back,
Recording briefly, "Lost."

But when the south wind stirs the
pools
And struggles in the lanes,
Her heart misgives her for her
vow,
And she pours soft refrains

Into the lap of adamant,
And spices, and the dew,
That stiffens quietly to quartz,
Upon her amber shoe.

XXIX.

The one that could repeat the
summer day
Were greater than itself, though
he
Minutest of mankind might be.
And who could reproduce the sun,
At period of going down —
The lingering and the stain, I mean
—
When Orient has been outgrown,
And Occident becomes unknown,
His name remain.

XXX - The Wind's Visit

The wind tapped like a tired man,
And like a host, "Come in,"
I boldly answered; entered then
My residence within

A rapid, footless guest,

To offer whom a chair
Were as impossible as hand
A sofa to the air.

No bone had he to bind him,
His speech was like the push
Of numerous humming-birds at
once
From a superior bush.

His countenance a billow,
His fingers, if he pass,
Let go a music, as of tunes
Blown tremulous in glass.

He visited, still flitting;
Then, like a timid man,
Again he tapped — 't was
flurriedly —
And I became alone.

XXXI.

Nature rarer uses yellow
    Than another hue;
Saves she all of that for sunsets, —
    Prodigal of blue,

Spending scarlet like a woman,
    Yellow she affords
Only scantly and selectly,
    Like a lover's words.

XXXII - Gossip

The leaves, like women,
interchange
    Sagacious confidence;

Somewhat of nods, and somewhat
of
    Portentous inference,

The parties in both cases
    Enjoining secrecy, —
Inviolable compact
    To notoriety.

XXXIII - Simplicity

How happy is the little stone
That rambles in the road alone,
And doesn't care about careers,
And exigencies never fears;
Whose coat of elemental brown
A passing universe put on;
And independent as the sun,
Associates or glows alone,
Fulfilling absolute decree
In casual simplicity.

XXXIV - Storm

It sounded as if the streets were
running,
And then the streets stood still.
Eclipse was all we could see at the
window,
And awe was all we could feel.

By and by the boldest stole out of
his covert,
To see if time was there.
Nature was in her beryl apron,
Mixing fresher air.

XXXV - The Rat

The rat is the concisest tenant.
He pays no rent, —
Repudiates the obligation,
On schemes intent.

Balking our wit
To sound or circumvent,
Hate cannot harm
A foe so reticent.

Neither decree
Prohibits him,
Lawful as
Equilibrium.

XXXVI.

Frequently the woods are pink,
Frequently are brown;
Frequently the hills undress
Behind my native town.

Oft a head is crested
I was wont to see,
And as oft a cranny
Where it used to be.

And the earth, they tell me,
On its axis turned, —
Wonderful rotation
By but twelve performed!

XXXVII - A Thunder-Storm

The wind begun to rock the grass
With threatening tunes and low,
—

He flung a menace at the earth,
A menace at the sky.

The leaves unhooked themselves
from trees
And started all abroad;
The dust did scoop itself like
hands
And throw away the road.

The wagons quickened on the
streets,
The thunder hurried slow;
The lightning showed a yellow
beak,
And then a livid claw.

The birds put up the bars to nests,
The cattle fled to barns;
There came one drop of giant rain,
And then, as if the hands

That held the dams had parted
hold,
The waters wrecked the sky,
But overlooked my father's house,
Just quartering a tree.

XXXVIII - With Flowers

South winds jostle them,
Bumblebees come,
Hover, hesitate,
Drink, and are gone.

Butterflies pause
On their passage Cashmere;
I, softly plucking,
Present them here!

XXXIX - Sunset

Where ships of purple gently toss
On seas of daffodil,
Fantastic sailors mingle,
And then — the wharf is still.

XL.

She sweeps with many-colored
brooms,
And leaves the shreds behind;
Oh, housewife in the evening west,
Come back, and dust the pond!

You dropped a purple ravelling in,
You dropped an amber thread;
And now you 've littered all the
East
With duds of emerald!

And still she plies her spotted
brooms,
And still the aprons fly,
Till brooms fade softly into stars
—
And then I come away.

XLI.

Like mighty footlights burned the
red
At bases of the trees, —
The far theatricals of day
Exhibiting to these.

'T was universe that did applaud
While, chiefest of the crowd,
Enabled by his royal dress,

Myself distinguished God.

XLII - Problems

Bring me the sunset in a cup,
Reckon the morning's flagons up,
    And say how many dew;
Tell me how far the morning leaps,
Tell me what time the weaver
sleeps
    Who spun the breadths of blue!

Write me how many notes there
be
In the new robin's ecstasy
    Among astonished boughs;
How many trips the tortoise
makes,
How many cups the bee partakes,
—
    The debauchee of dews!

Also, who laid the rainbow's piers,
Also, who leads the docile spheres
    By withes of supple blue?
Whose fingers string the stalactite,
Who counts the wampum of the
night,
    To see that none is due?

Who built this little Alban house
And shut the windows down so
close
    My spirit cannot see?
Who 'll let me out some gala day,
With implements to fly away,
    Passing pomposity?

XLIII - The Juggler Of Day

Blazing in gold and quenching in
purple,
Leaping like leopards to the sky,
Then at the feet of the old horizon
Laying her spotted face, to die;
Stooping as low as the otter's
window,
Touching the roof and tinting the
barn,
Kissing her bonnet to the meadow,
—
And the juggler of day is gone!

XLIV - My Cricket

Farther in summer than the birds,
Pathetic from the grass,
A minor nation celebrates
Its unobtrusive mass.

No ordinance is seen,
So gradual the grace,
A pensive custom it becomes,
Enlarging loneliness.

Antiquest felt at noon
When August, burning low,
Calls forth this spectral canticle,
Repose to typify.

Remit as yet no grace,
No furrow on the glow,
Yet a druidic difference
Enhances nature now.

XLV.

As imperceptibly as grief
The summer lapsed away, —
Too imperceptible, at last,
To seem like perfidy.

A quietness distilled,
As twilight long begun,
Or Nature, spending with herself
Sequestered afternoon.

The dusk drew earlier in,
The morning foreign shone, —
A courteous, yet harrowing grace,
As guest who would be gone.

And thus, without a wing,
Or service of a keel,
Our summer made her light
escape
Into the beautiful.

XLVI.

It can't be summer, — that got
through;
It 's early yet for spring;
There 's that long town of white to
cross
Before the blackbirds sing.

It can't be dying, — it's too rouge,
—
The dead shall go in white.
So sunset shuts my question down
With clasps of chrysolite.

XLVII - Summer's Obsequies

The gentian weaves her fringes,
The maple's loom is red.
My departing blossoms
Obviate parade.

A brief, but patient illness,
An hour to prepare;
And one, below this morning,
Is where the angels are.

It was a short procession, —
The bobolink was there,
An aged bee addressed us,
And then we knelt in prayer.

We trust that she was willing, —
We ask that we may be.
Summer, sister, seraph,
Let us go with thee!

In the name of the bee
And of the butterfly
And of the breeze, amen!

XLVIII - Fringed Gentian

God made a little gentian;
It tried to be a rose
And failed, and all the summer
laughed.
But just before the snows
There came a purple creature
That ravished all the hill;
And summer hid her forehead,
And mockery was still.
The frosts were her condition;
The Tyrian would not come
Until the North evoked it.

"Creator! shall I bloom?"

XLIX - November

Besides the autumn poets sing,
A few prosaic days
A little this side of the snow
And that side of the haze.

A few incisive mornings,
A few ascetic eyes, —
Gone Mr. Bryant's golden-rod,
And Mr. Thomson's sheaves.

Still is the bustle in the brook,
Sealed are the spicy valves;
Mesmeric fingers softly touch
The eyes of many elves.

Perhaps a squirrel may remain,
My sentiments to share.
Grant me, O Lord, a sunny mind,
Thy windy will to bear!

L - The Snow

It sifts from leaden sieves,
It powders all the wood,
It fills with alabaster wool
The wrinkles of the road.

It makes an even face
Of mountain and of plain, —
Unbroken forehead from the east
Unto the east again.

It reaches to the fence,
It wraps it, rail by rail,
Till it is lost in fleeces;

It flings a crystal veil

On stump and stack and stem, —
The summer's empty room,
Acres of seams where harvests
were,
Recordless, but for them.

It ruffles wrists of posts,
As ankles of a queen, —
Then stills its artisans like ghosts,
Denying they have been.

His character a tonic,
His future a dispute;
Unfair an immortality
That leaves this neighbor out.

LI - The Blue Jay

No brigadier throughout the year
So civic as the jay.
A neighbor and a warrior too,
With shrill felicity

Pursuing winds that censure us
A February day,
The brother of the universe
Was never blown away.

The snow and he are intimate;
I 've often seen them play
When heaven looked upon us all
With such severity,

I felt apology were due
To an insulted sky,
Whose pompous frown was
nutriment
To their temerity.

The pillow of this daring head
Is pungent evergreens;
His larder — terse and militant —
Unknown, refreshing things;

IV. Time and Eternity

I.

Let down the bars, O Death!
The tired flocks come in
Whose bleating ceases to repeat,
Whose wandering is done.

Thine is the stillest night,
Thine the securest fold;
Too near thou art for seeking thee,
Too tender to be told.

II.

Going to heaven!
I don't know when,
Pray do not ask me how, —
Indeed, I 'm too astonished
To think of answering you!
Going to heaven! —
How dim it sounds!
And yet it will be done
As sure as flocks go home at night
Unto the shepherd's arm!

Perhaps you 're going too!
Who knows?
If you should get there first,
Save just a little place for me
Close to the two I lost!

The smallest "robe" will fit me,
And just a bit of "crown;"
For you know we do not mind our
dress
When we are going home.

I 'm glad I don't believe it,
For it would stop my breath,
And I 'd like to look a little more
At such a curious earth!
I am glad they did believe it
Whom I have never found
Since the mighty autumn
afternoon
I left them in the ground.

III.

At least to pray is left, is left.
O Jesus! in the air
I know not which thy chamber is,
—
I 'm knocking everywhere.

Thou stirrest earthquake in the
South,
And maelstrom in the sea;
Say, Jesus Christ of Nazareth,
Hast thou no arm for me?

IV - Epitaph

Step lightly on this narrow spot!
The broadest land that grows
Is not so ample as the breast
These emerald seams enclose.

Step lofty; for this name is told
As far as cannon dwell,
Or flag subsist, or fame export
Her deathless syllable.

V.

Morns like these we parted;

Noons like these she rose,
Fluttering first, then firmer,
To her fair repose.

Never did she lisp it,
And 't was not for me;
She was mute from transport,
I, from agony!

Till the evening, nearing,
One the shutters drew —
Quick! a sharper rustling!
And this linnet flew!

VI.

A death-blow is a life-blow to
some
Who, till they died, did not alive
become;
Who, had they lived, had died, but
when
They died, vitality begun.

VII.

I read my sentence steadily,
Reviewed it with my eyes,
To see that I made no mistake
In its extremest clause, —

The date, and manner of the
shame;
And then the pious form
That "God have mercy" on the soul
The jury voted him.

I made my soul familiar
With her extremity,

That at the last it should not be
A novel agony,

But she and Death, acquainted,
Meet tranquilly as friends,
Salute and pass without a hint —
And there the matter ends.

VIII.

I have not told my garden yet,
Lest that should conquer me;
I have not quite the strength now
To break it to the bee.

I will not name it in the street,
For shops would stare, that I,
So shy, so very ignorant,
Should have the face to die.

The hillsides must not know it,
Where I have rambled so,
Nor tell the loving forests
The day that I shall go,

Nor lisp it at the table,
Nor heedless by the way
Hint that within the riddle
One will walk to-day!

IX - The Battle-Field

They dropped like flakes, they
dropped like stars,
   Like petals from a rose,
When suddenly across the June
   A wind with fingers goes.

They perished in the seamless
grass, —
    No eye could find the place;
But God on his repealless list
    Can summon every face.

X.

The only ghost I ever saw
Was dressed in mechlin, — so;
He wore no sandal on his foot,
And stepped like flakes of snow.
His gait was soundless, like the
bird,
But rapid, like the roe;
His fashions quaint, mosaic,
Or, haply, mistletoe.

His conversation seldom,
His laughter like the breeze
That dies away in dimples
Among the pensive trees.
Our interview was transient,—
Of me, himself was shy;
And God forbid I look behind
Since that appalling day!

XI.

Some, too fragile for winter winds,
The thoughtful grave encloses, —
Tenderly tucking them in from
frost
Before their feet are cold.

Never the treasures in her nest
The cautious grave exposes,
Building where schoolboy dare
not look

And sportsman is not bold.

This covert have all the children
Early aged, and often cold, —
Sparrows unnoticed by the Father;
Lambs for whom time had not a
fold.

XII.

As by the dead we love to sit,
Become so wondrous dear,
As for the lost we grapple,
Though all the rest are here, —

In broken mathematics
We estimate our prize,
Vast, in its fading ratio,
To our penurious eyes!

XIII - Memorials

Death sets a thing significant
The eye had hurried by,
Except a perished creature
Entreat us tenderly

To ponder little workmanships
In crayon or in wool,
With "This was last her fingers
did,"
Industrious until

The thimble weighed too heavy,
The stitches stopped themselves,
And then 't was put among the
dust
Upon the closet shelves.

A book I have, a friend gave,
Whose pencil, here and there,
Had notched the place that
pleased him, —
At rest his fingers are.

Now, when I read, I read not,
For interrupting tears
Obliterate the etchings
Too costly for repairs.

XIV.

I went to heaven, —
'T was a small town,
Lit with a ruby,
Lathed with down.
Stiller than the fields
At the full dew,
Beautiful as pictures
No man drew.
People like the moth,
Of mechlin, frames,
Duties of gossamer,
And eider names.
Almost contented
I could be
'Mong such unique
Society.

XV.

Their height in heaven comforts
not,
Their glory nought to me;
'T was best imperfect, as it was;
I 'm finite, I can't see.

The house of supposition,

The glimmering frontier
That skirts the acres of perhaps,
To me shows insecure.

The wealth I had contented me;
If 't was a meaner size,
Then I had counted it until
It pleased my narrow eyes

Better than larger values,
However true their show;
This timid life of evidence
Keeps pleading, "I don't know."

XVI.

There is a shame of nobleness
Confronting sudden pelf, —
A finer shame of ecstasy
Convicted of itself.

A best disgrace a brave man feels,
Acknowledged of the brave, —
One more "Ye Blessed" to be told;
But this involves the grave.

XVII - Triumph

Triumph may be of several kinds.
There 's triumph in the room
When that old imperator, Death,
By faith is overcome.

There 's triumph of the finer mind
When truth, affronted long,
Advances calm to her supreme,
Her God her only throng.

A triumph when temptation's bribe
Is slowly handed back,
One eye upon the heaven renounced
And one upon the rack.

Severer triumph, by himself
Experienced, who can pass
Acquitted from that naked bar,
Jehovah's countenance!

XVIII.

Pompless no life can pass away;
    The lowliest career
To the same pageant wends its way
    As that exalted here.
How cordial is the mystery!
    The hospitable pall
A "this way" beckons spaciously, —
    A miracle for all!

XIX.

I noticed people disappeared,
When but a little child, —
Supposed they visited remote,
Or settled regions wild.

Now know I they both visited
And settled regions wild,
But did because they died, — a fact
Withheld the little child!

XX - Following

I had no cause to be awake,
My best was gone to sleep,
And morn a new politeness took,
And failed to wake them up,

But called the others clear,
And passed their curtains by.
Sweet morning, when I over-sleep,
Knock, recollect, for me!

I looked at sunrise once,
And then I looked at them,
And wishfulness in me arose
For circumstance the same.

'T was such an ample peace,
It could not hold a sigh, —
'T was Sabbath with the bells divorced,
'T was sunset all the day.
So choosing but a gown
And taking but a prayer,
The only raiment I should need,
I struggled, and was there.

XXI.

If anybody's friend be dead,
It 's sharpest of the theme
The thinking how they walked alive,
At such and such a time.

Their costume, of a Sunday,
Some manner of the hair, —
A prank nobody knew but them,
Lost, in the sepulchre.

How warm they were on such a
day:
You almost feel the date,
So short way off it seems; and
now,
They 're centuries from that.

How pleased they were at what
you said;
You try to touch the smile,
And dip your fingers in the frost:
When was it, can you tell,

You asked the company to tea,
Acquaintance, just a few,
And chatted close with this grand
thing
That don't remember you?

Past bows and invitations,
Past interview, and vow,
Past what ourselves can estimate,
—
That makes the quick of woe!

XXII - The Journey

Our journey had advanced;
Our feet were almost come
To that odd fork in Being's road,
Eternity by term.

Our pace took sudden awe,
Our feet reluctant led.
Before were cities, but between,
The forest of the dead.

Retreat was out of hope, —
Behind, a sealed route,
Eternity's white flag before,

And God at every gate.

XXIII - A Country Burial

Ample make this bed.
Make this bed with awe;
In it wait till judgment break
Excellent and fair.

Be its mattress straight,
Be its pillow round;
Let no sunrise' yellow noise
Interrupt this ground.

XXIV - Going

On such a night, or such a night,
Would anybody care
If such a little figure
Slipped quiet from its chair,

So quiet, oh, how quiet!
That nobody might know
But that the little figure
Rocked softer, to and fro?
On such a dawn, or such a dawn,
Would anybody sigh
That such a little figure
Too sound asleep did lie

For chanticleer to wake it, —
Or stirring house below,
Or giddy bird in orchard,
Or early task to do?

There was a little figure plump
For every little knoll,
Busy needles, and spools of
thread,

And trudging feet from school.

Playmates, and holidays, and nuts,
And visions vast and small.
Strange that the feet so precious
charged
Should reach so small a goal!

XXV.

Essential oils are wrung:
The attar from the rose
Is not expressed by suns alone,
It is the gift of screws.

The general rose decays;
But this, in lady's drawer,
Makes summer when the lady lies
In ceaseless rosemary.

XXVI.

I lived on dread; to those who
know
The stimulus there is
In danger, other impetus
Is numb and vital-less.

As 't were a spur upon the soul,
A fear will urge it where
To go without the spectre's aid
Were challenging despair.

XXVII.

If I should die,
And you should live,
And time should gurgle on,
And morn should beam,

And noon should burn,
As it has usual done;
If birds should build as early,
And bees as bustling go, —
One might depart at option
From enterprise below!
'T is sweet to know that stocks
will stand
When we with daisies lie,
That commerce will continue,
And trades as briskly fly.
It makes the parting tranquil
And keeps the soul serene,
That gentlemen so sprightly
Conduct the pleasing scene!

XXVIII - At Length

Her final summer was it,
And yet we guessed it not;
If tenderer industriousness
Pervaded her, we thought

A further force of life
Developed from within, —
When Death lit all the shortness
up,
And made the hurry plain.

We wondered at our blindness, —
When nothing was to see
But her Carrara guide-post, —
At our stupidity,

When, duller than our dulness,
The busy darling lay,
So busy was she, finishing,
So leisurely were we!

XXIX - Ghosts

One need not be a chamber to be
haunted,
One need not be a house;
The brain has corridors
surpassing
Material place.

Far safer, of a midnight meeting
External ghost,
Than an interior confronting
That whiter host.

Far safer through an Abbey gallop,
The stones achase,
Than, moonless, one's own self
encounter
In lonesome place.

Ourself, behind ourself concealed,
Should startle most;
Assassin, hid in our apartment,
Be horror's least.

The prudent carries a revolver,
He bolts the door,
O'erlooking a superior spectre
More near.

XXX - Vanished

She died, — this was the way she
died;
And when her breath was done,
Took up her simple wardrobe
And started for the sun.

Her little figure at the gate
The angels must have spied,
Since I could never find her
Upon the mortal side.

XXXI - Precedence

Wait till the majesty of Death
Invests so mean a brow!
Almost a powdered footman
Might dare to touch it now!

Wait till in everlasting robes
This democrat is dressed,
Then prate about "preferment"
And "station" and the rest!

Around this quiet courtier
Obsequious angels wait!
Full royal is his retinue,
Full purple is his state!

A lord might dare to lift the hat
To such a modest clay,
Since that my Lord, "the Lord of
lords"
Receives unblushingly!

XXXII - Gone

Went up a year this evening!
I recollect it well!
Amid no bells nor bravos
The bystanders will tell!
Cheerful, as to the village,
Tranquil, as to repose,
Chastened, as to the chapel,
This humble tourist rose.
Did not talk of returning,
Alluded to no time
When, were the gales propitious,

We might look for him;
Was grateful for the roses
In life's diverse bouquet,
Talked softly of new species
To pick another day.

Beguiling thus the wonder,
The wondrous nearer drew;
Hands bustled at the moorings —
The crowd respectful grew.
Ascended from our vision
To countenances new!
A difference, a daisy,
Is all the rest I knew!

XXXIII - Requiem

Taken from men this morning,
Carried by men to-day,
Met by the gods with banners
Who marshalled her away.

One little maid from playmates,
One little mind from school, —
There must be guests in Eden;
All the rooms are full.

Far as the east from even,
Dim as the border star, —
Courtiers quaint, in kingdoms,
Our departed are.

XXXIV.

What inn is this
Where for the night
Peculiar traveller comes?
Who is the landlord?
Where the maids?

Behold, what curious rooms!
No ruddy fires on the hearth,
No brimming tankards flow.
Necromancer, landlord,
Who are these below?

XXXV.

It was not death, for I stood up,
And all the dead lie down;
It was not night, for all the bells
Put out their tongues, for noon.

It was not frost, for on my flesh
I felt siroccos crawl, —
Nor fire, for just my marble feet
Could keep a chancel cool.

And yet it tasted like them all;
The figures I have seen
Set orderly, for burial,
Reminded me of mine,

As if my life were shaven
And fitted to a frame,
And could not breathe without a
key;
And 't was like midnight, some,

When everything that ticked has
stopped,
And space stares, all around,
Or grisly frosts, first autumn
morns,
Repeal the beating ground.
But most like chaos, — stopless,
cool, —
Without a chance or spar,
Or even a report of land
To justify despair.

XXXVI - Till The End

I should not dare to leave my
friend,
Because — because if he should
die
While I was gone, and I — too late
—
Should reach the heart that
wanted me;

If I should disappoint the eyes
That hunted, hunted so, to see,
And could not bear to shut until
They "noticed" me — they noticed
me;

If I should stab the patient faith
So sure I 'd come — so sure I 'd
come,
It listening, listening, went to sleep
Telling my tardy name, —

My heart would wish it broke
before,
Since breaking then, since
breaking then,
Were useless as next morning's
sun,
Where midnight frosts had lain!

XXXVII - Void

Great streets of silence led away
To neighborhoods of pause;
Here was no notice, no dissent,
No universe, no laws.
By clocks 't was morning, and for
night
The bells at distance called;

But epoch had no basis here,
For period exhaled.

XXXVIII.

A throe upon the features
A hurry in the breath,
An ecstasy of parting
Denominated "Death," —

An anguish at the mention,
Which, when to patience grown,
I 've known permission given
To rejoin its own.

XXXIX - Saved!

Of tribulation these are they
Denoted by the white;
The spangled gowns, a lesser rank
Of victors designate.

All these did conquer; but the ones
Who overcame most times
Wear nothing commoner than
snow,
No ornament but palms.

Surrender is a sort unknown
On this superior soil;
Defeat, an outgrown anguish,
Remembered as the mile

Our panting ankle barely gained
When night devoured the road;
But we stood whispering in the
house,
And all we said was "Saved"!

XL.

I think just how my shape will rise
When I shall be forgiven,
Till hair and eyes and timid head
Are out of sight, in heaven.

I think just how my lips will weigh
With shapeless, quivering prayer
That you, so late, consider me,
The sparrow of your care.

I mind me that of anguish sent,
Some drifts were moved away
Before my simple bosom broke, —
And why not this, if they?

And so, until delirious borne
I con that thing, — "forgiven," —
Till with long fright and longer
trust
I drop my heart, unshriven!

XLI - The Forgotten Grave

After a hundred years
Nobody knows the place, —
Agony, that enacted there,
Motionless as peace.

Weeds triumphant ranged,
Strangers strolled and spelled
At the lone orthography
Of the elder dead.

Winds of summer fields
Recollect the way, —
Instinct picking up the key
Dropped by memory.

XLII.

Lay this laurel on the one
Too intrinsic for renown.
Laurel! veil your deathless tree, —
Him you chasten, that is he!

Poems by Emily Dickinson - Third Series

Edited by Mabel Loomis Todd

It's all I have to bring to-day,
  This, and my heart beside,
This, and my heart, and all the fields,
  And all the meadows wide.
Be sure you count, should I forget, —
  Some one the sum could tell, —
This, and my heart, and all the bees
  Which in the clover dwell.

Preface

The intellectual activity of Emily Dickinson was so great that a large and characteristic choice is still possible among her literary material, and this third volume of her verses is put forth in response to the repeated wish of the admirers of her peculiar genius. Much of Emily Dickinson's prose was rhythmic, —even rhymed, though frequently not set apart in lines.

Also many verses, written as such, were sent to friends in letters; these were published in 1894, in the volumes of her Letters. It has not been necessary, however, to include them in this Series, and all have been omitted, except three or four exceptionally strong ones, as "A Book," and "With Flowers."

There is internal evidence that many of the poems were simply spontaneous flashes of insight, apparently unrelated to outward circumstance. Others, however, had an obvious personal origin; for example, the verses "I had a Guinea golden," which seem to have been sent to some friend travelling in Europe, as a dainty reminder of letter-writing delinquencies. The surroundings in which any of Emily Dickinson's verses are known to have been written usually serve to explain them clearly; but in general the present volume is full of thoughts needing no interpretation to those who apprehend this scintillating spirit.

M. L. T.

Amherst, October, 1896.

I. Life

I - Real Riches

'T is little I could care for pearls
  Who own the ample sea;
Or brooches, when the Emperor
  With rubies pelteth me;

Or gold, who am the Prince of
Mines;
  Or diamonds, when I see
A diadem to fit a dome
  Continual crowning me.

II - Superiority To Fate

Superiority to fate
  Is difficult to learn.
'T is not conferred by any,
  But possible to earn

A pittance at a time,
  Until, to her surprise,
The soul with strict economy
  Subsists till Paradise.

III - Hope

Hope is a subtle glutton;
  He feeds upon the fair;
And yet, inspected closely,
  What abstinence is there!

His is the halcyon table
  That never seats but one,
And whatsoever is consumed
The same amounts remain.

IV - Forbidden Fruit

I.

Forbidden fruit a flavor has
  That lawful orchards mocks;
How luscious lies the pea within
  The pod that Duty locks!

V - Forbidden Fruit

II.

Heaven is what I cannot reach!
  The apple on the tree,
Provided it do hopeless hang,
  That 'heaven' is, to me.

The color on the cruising cloud,
  The interdicted ground
Behind the hill, the house behind,
—
  There Paradise is found!

VI - A Word

A word is dead
When it is said,
  Some say.
I say it just
Begins to live
  That day.

VII.

To venerate the simple days
  Which lead the seasons by,
Needs but to remember
  That from you or me
They may take the trifle
  Termed mortality!

To invest existence with a stately
air,
Needs but to remember
  That the acorn there
Is the egg of forests
  For the upper air!

VIII - Life's Trades

It's such a little thing to weep,
  So short a thing to sigh;
And yet by trades the size of these
  We men and women die!

IX.

Drowning is not so pitiful
  As the attempt to rise.
Three times, 't is said, a sinking
man
  Comes up to face the skies,
And then declines forever
  To that abhorred abode
Where hope and he part company,
—
  For he is grasped of God.
The Maker's cordial visage,
  However good to see,
Is shunned, we must admit it,
  Like an adversity.

X.

How still the bells in steeples
stand,
  Till, swollen with the sky,
They leap upon their silver feet
  In frantic melody!

XI.

If the foolish call them 'flowers,'
  Need the wiser tell?
If the savans 'classify' them,
  It is just as well!

Those who read the Revelations
  Must not criticise
Those who read the same edition
  With beclouded eyes!

Could we stand with that old
Moses
  Canaan denied, —
Scan, like him, the stately
landscape
  On the other side, —

Doubtless we should deem
superfluous
  Many sciences
Not pursued by learnèd angels
  In scholastic skies!

Low amid that glad Belles lettres
  Grant that we may stand,
Stars, amid profound Galaxies,
  At that grand 'Right hand'!

XII - A Syllable

Could mortal lip divine
  The undeveloped freight
Of a delivered syllable,
  'T would crumble with the
weight.

XIII - Parting

My life closed twice before its
close;
  It yet remains to see
If Immortality unveil
  A third event to me,

So huge, so hopeless to conceive,
  As these that twice befell.
Parting is all we know of heaven,
  And all we need of hell.

XIV - Aspiration

We never know how high we are
  Till we are called to rise;
And then, if we are true to plan,
  Our statures touch the skies.

The heroism we recite
  Would be a daily thing,
Did not ourselves the cubits warp
  For fear to be a king.

XV - The Inevitable

While I was fearing it, it came,
  But came with less of fear,
Because that fearing it so long

Had almost made it dear.
There is a fitting a dismay,
  A fitting a despair.
'Tis harder knowing it is due,
  Than knowing it is here.
The trying on the utmost,
  The morning it is new,
Is terribler than wearing it
  A whole existence through.

XVI - A Book

There is no frigate like a book
  To take us lands away,
Nor any coursers like a page
  Of prancing poetry.
This traverse may the poorest
take
  Without oppress of toll;
How frugal is the chariot
  That bears a human soul!

XVII.

Who has not found the heaven
below
  Will fail of it above.
God's residence is next to mine,
  His furniture is love.

XVIII - A Portrait

A face devoid of love or grace,
  A hateful, hard, successful face,
A face with which a stone
  Would feel as thoroughly at ease
As were they old acquaintances,
—
  First time together thrown.

XIX - I Had a Guinea Golden

I had a guinea golden;
　I lost it in the sand,
And though the sum was simple,
　And pounds were in the land,
Still had it such a value
　Unto my frugal eye,
That when I could not find it
　I sat me down to sigh.

I had a crimson robin
　Who sang full many a day,
But when the woods were painted
　He, too, did fly away.
Time brought me other robins, —
　Their ballads were the same, —
Still for my missing troubadour
　I kept the 'house at hame.'

I had a star in heaven;
　One Pleiad was its name,
And when I was not heeding
　It wandered from the same.
And though the skies are crowded,
　And all the night ashine,
I do not care about it,
　Since none of them are mine.

My story has a moral:
　I have a missing friend, —
Pleiad its name, and robin,
　And guinea in the sand, —
And when this mournful ditty,
　Accompanied with tear,
Shall meet the eye of traitor
　In country far from here,
Grant that repentance solemn
　May seize upon his mind,
And he no consolation
　Beneath the sun may find.

NOTE. — This poem may have had, like many others, a personal origin. It is more than probable that it was sent to some friend travelling in Europe, a dainty reminder of letter writing delinquencies.

XX - Saturday Afternoon

From all the jails the boys and girls
　Ecstatically leap, —
Beloved, only afternoon
　That prison doesn't keep.

They storm the earth and stun the air,
　A mob of solid bliss.
Alas! that frowns could lie in wait
　For such a foe as this!

XXI.

Few get enough, — enough is one;
　To that ethereal throng
Have not each one of us the right
　To stealthily belong?

XXII.

Upon the gallows hung a wretch,
　Too sullied for the hell
To which the law entitled him.
　As nature's curtain fell
The one who bore him tottered in,
　For this was woman's son.
''T was all I had,' she stricken gasped;
　Oh, what a livid boon!

XXIII - The Lost Thought

I felt a clearing in my mind
  As if my brain had split;
I tried to match it, seam by seam,
  But could not make them fit.

The thought behind I strove to join
  Unto the thought before,
But sequence ravelled out of reach
  Like balls upon a floor.

XXIV - Reticence

The reticent volcano keeps
  His never slumbering plan;
Confided are his projects pink
  To no precarious man.

If nature will not tell the tale
  Jehovah told to her,
Can human nature not survive
  Without a listener?

Admonished by her buckled lips
  Let every babbler be.
The only secret people keep
  Is Immortality.

XXV - With Flowers

If recollecting were forgetting,
  Then I remember not;
And if forgetting, recollecting,
  How near I had forgot!
And if to miss were merry,
  And if to mourn were gay,
How very blithe the fingers
  That gathered these to-day!

XXVI.

The farthest thunder that I heard
  Was nearer than the sky,
And rumbles still, though torrid noons
  Have lain their missiles by.
The lightning that preceded it
  Struck no one but myself,
But I would not exchange the bolt
  For all the rest of life.
Indebtedness to oxygen
  The chemist may repay,
But not the obligation
  To electricity.
It founds the homes and decks the days,
  And every clamor bright
Is but the gleam concomitant
  Of that waylaying light.
The thought is quiet as a flake, —
  A crash without a sound;
How life's reverberation
  Its explanation found!

XXVII.

On the bleakness of my lot
  Bloom I strove to raise.
Late, my acre of a rock
  Yielded grape and maize.

Soil of flint if steadfast tilled
  Will reward the hand;
Seed of palm by Lybian sun
  Fructified in sand.

XXVIII - Contrast

A door just opened on a street —
  I, lost, was passing by —
An instant's width of warmth disclosed,
  And wealth, and company.

The door as sudden shut, and I,
  I, lost, was passing by, —
Lost doubly, but by contrast most,
  Enlightening misery.

XXIX - Friends

Are friends delight or pain?
  Could bounty but remain
Riches were good.

But if they only stay
Bolder to fly away,
  Riches are sad.

XXX - Fire

Ashes denote that fire was;
  Respect the grayest pile
For the departed creature's sake
  That hovered there awhile.

Fire exists the first in light,
  And then consolidates, —
Only the chemist can disclose
  Into what carbonates.

XXXI - A Man

Fate slew him, but he did not drop;
  She felled — he did not fall —
Impaled him on her fiercest stakes —
  He neutralized them all.

She stung him, sapped his firm advance,
  But, when her worst was done,
And he, unmoved, regarded her,
  Acknowledged him a man.

XXXII - Ventures

Finite to fail, but infinite to venture.
  For the one ship that struts the shore
Many's the gallant, overwhelmed creature
  Nodding in navies nevermore.

XXXIII - Griefs

I measure every grief I meet
  With analytic eyes;
I wonder if it weighs like mine,
  Or has an easier size.

I wonder if they bore it long,
  Or did it just begin?
I could not tell the date of mine,
  It feels so old a pain.

I wonder if it hurts to live,
  And if they have to try,
And whether, could they choose between,
  They would not rather die.

I wonder if when years have piled
—
   Some thousands — on the cause
Of early hurt, if such a lapse
   Could give them any pause;

Or would they go on aching still
   Through centuries above,
Enlightened to a larger pain
   By contrast with the love.

The grieved are many, I am told;
   The reason deeper lies, —
Death is but one and comes but
once,
   And only nails the eyes.

There's grief of want, and grief of
cold, —
   A sort they call 'despair;'
There's banishment from native
eyes,
   In sight of native air.

And though I may not guess the
kind
   Correctly, yet to me
A piercing comfort it affords
   In passing Calvary,

To note the fashions of the cross,
   Of those that stand alone,
Still fascinated to presume
   That some are like my own.

XXXIV.

I have a king who does not speak;
So, wondering, thro' the hours
meek

I trudge the day away,—
Half glad when it is night and
sleep,
If, haply, thro' a dream to peep
   In parlors shut by day.

And if I do, when morning comes,
It is as if a hundred drums
   Did round my pillow roll,
And shouts fill all my childish sky,
And bells keep saying 'victory'
   From steeples in my soul!

And if I don't, the little Bird
Within the Orchard is not heard,
   And I·omit to pray,
'Father, thy will be done' to-day,
For my will goes the other way,
   And it were perjury!

XXXV - Disenchantment

It dropped so low in my regard
   I heard it hit the ground,
And go to pieces on the stones
   At bottom of my mind;

Yet blamed the fate that fractured,
less
   Than I reviled myself
For entertaining plated wares
   Upon my silver shelf.

XXXVI - Lost Faith

To lose one's faith surpasses
   The loss of an estate,
Because estates can be
   Replenished, — faith cannot.

Inherited with life,
  Belief but once can be;
Annihilate a single clause,
  And Being's beggary.

XXXVII - Lost Joy

I had a daily bliss
  I half indifferent viewed,
Till sudden I perceived it stir, —
  It grew as I pursued,

Till when, around a crag,
  It wasted from my sight,
Enlarged beyond my utmost
scope,
  I learned its sweetness right.

XXXVIII.

I worked for chaff, and earning
wheat
  Was haughty and betrayed.
What right had fields to arbitrate
  In matters ratified?

I tasted wheat, — and hated chaff,
  And thanked the ample friend;
Wisdom is more becoming viewed
  At distance than at hand.

XXXIX.

Life, and Death, and Giants
  Such as these, are still.
Minor apparatus, hopper of the
mill,
Beetle at the candle,
  Or a fife's small fame,

Maintain by accident
  That they proclaim.

XL - Alpine Glow

Our lives are Swiss, —
  So still, so cool,
  Till, some odd afternoon,
The Alps neglect their curtains,
  And we look farther on.

Italy stands the other side,
  While, like a guard between,
The solemn Alps,
The siren Alps,
  Forever intervene!

XLI - Remembrance

Remembrance has a rear and
front, —
  'T is something like a house;
It has a garret also
  For refuse and the mouse,

Besides, the deepest cellar
  That ever mason hewed;
Look to it, by its fathoms
  Ourselves be not pursued.

XLII.

To hang our head ostensibly,
  And subsequent to find
That such was not the posture
  Of our immortal mind,

Affords the sly presumption

That, in so dense a fuzz,
You, too, take cobweb attitudes
    Upon a plane of gauze!

XLIII - The Brain

The brain is wider than the sky,
    For, put them side by side,
The one the other will include
    With ease, and you beside.

The brain is deeper than the sea,
    For, hold them, blue to blue,
The one the other will absorb,
    As sponges, buckets do.

The brain is just the weight of God,
    For, lift them, pound for pound,
And they will differ, if they do,
    As syllable from sound.

XLIV.

The bone that has no marrow;
    What ultimate for that?
It is not fit for table,
    For beggar, or for cat.

A bone has obligations,
    A being has the same;
A marrowless assembly
    Is culpabler than shame.

But how shall finished creatures
    A function fresh obtain? —
Old Nicodemus' phantom
    Confronting us again!

XLV - The Past

The past is such a curious
creature,
    To look her in the face
A transport may reward us,
    Or a disgrace.

Unarmed if any meet her,
    I charge him, fly!
Her rusty ammunition
    Might yet reply!

XLVI.

To help our bleaker parts
    Salubrious hours are given,
Which if they do not fit for earth
    Drill silently for heaven.

XLVII.

What soft, cherubic creatures
    These gentlewomen are!
One would as soon assault a plush
    Or violate a star.

Such dimity convictions,
    A horror so refined
Of freckled human nature,
    Of Deity ashamed, —

It's such a common glory,
    A fisherman's degree!
Redemption, brittle lady,
    Be so, ashamed of thee.

XLVIII - Desire

Who never wanted, — maddest
joy
  Remains to him unknown:
The banquet of abstemiousness
  Surpasses that of wine.

Within its hope, though yet
ungrasped
  Desire's perfect goal,
No nearer, lest reality
  Should disenthrall thy soul.

XLIX - Philosophy

It might be easier
  To fail with land in sight,
Than gain my blue peninsula
  To perish of delight.

L - Power

You cannot put a fire out;
  A thing that can ignite
Can go, itself, without a fan
  Upon the slowest night.

You cannot fold a flood
  And put it in a drawer, —
Because the winds would find it
out,
  And tell your cedar floor.

LI.

A modest lot, a fame petite,

A brief campaign of sting and
sweet
  Is plenty! Is enough!
A sailor's business is the shore,
  A soldier's — balls. Who asketh
more
Must seek the neighboring life!

LII.

Is bliss, then, such abyss
I must not put my foot amiss
For fear I spoil my shoe?

I'd rather suit my foot
Than save my boot,
For yet to buy another pair
Is possible
At any fair.

But bliss is sold just once;
The patent lost
None buy it any more.

LIII - Experience

I stepped from plank to plank
  So slow and cautiously;
The stars about my head I felt,
  About my feet the sea.

I knew not but the next
  Would be my final inch, —
This gave me that precarious gait
  Some call experience.

LIV - Thanksgiving Day

One day is there of the series

Termed Thanksgiving day,
Celebrated part at table,
  Part in memory.

Neither patriarch nor pussy,
  I dissect the play;
Seems it, to my hooded thinking,
  Reflex holiday.

Had there been no sharp
subtraction
  From the early sum,
Not an acre or a caption
  Where was once a room,

Not a mention, whose small
pebble
  Wrinkled any bay, —
Unto such, were such assembly,
  'T were Thanksgiving day.

LV - Childish Griefs

Softened by Time's consummate
plush,
  How sleek the woe appears
That threatened childhood's
citadel
  And undermined the years!
Bisected now by bleaker griefs,
  We envy the despair
That devastated childhood's
realm,
  So easy to repair.

II. Love

I - Consecration

Proud of my broken heart since
thou didst break it,
  Proud of the pain I did not feel
till thee,
Proud of my night since thou with
moons dost slake it,
  Not to partake thy passion, my
humility.

II - Love's Humility

My worthiness is all my doubt,
  His merit all my fear,
Contrasting which, my qualities
  Do lowlier appear;

Lest I should insufficient prove
  For his beloved need,
The chiefest apprehension
  Within my loving creed.

So I, the undivine abode
  Of his elect content,
Conform my soul as 't were a
church
  Unto her sacrament.

III - Love

Love is anterior to life,
  Posterior to death,
Initial of creation, and
  The exponent of breath.

IV - Satisfied

One blessing had I, than the rest
  So larger to my eyes
That I stopped gauging, satisfied,
  For this enchanted size.

It was the limit of my dream,
  The focus of my prayer, —
A perfect, paralyzing bliss
  Contented as despair.

I knew no more of want or cold,
  Phantasms both become,
For this new value in the soul,
  Supremest earthly sum.

The heaven below the heaven
above
  Obscured with ruddier hue.
Life's latitude leant over-full;
  The judgment perished, too.

Why joys so scantily disburse,
  Why Paradise defer,
Why floods are served to us in
bowls, —
  I speculate no more.

V - With A Flower

When roses cease to bloom, dear,
  And violets are done,
When bumble-bees in solemn
flight
  Have passed beyond the sun,

The hand that paused to gather
  Upon this summer's day
Will idle lie, in Auburn, —

Then take my flower, pray!

VI - Song

Summer for thee grant I may be
    When summer days are flown!
Thy music still when whippoorwill
    And oriole are done!

For thee to bloom, I'll skip the
tomb
    And sow my blossoms o'er!
Pray gather me, Anemone,
    Thy flower forevermore!

VII - Loyalty

Split the lark and you'll find the
music,
    Bulb after bulb, in silver rolled,
Scantily dealt to the summer
morning,
    Saved for your ear when lutes be
old.

Loose the flood, you shall find it
patent,
    Gush after gush, reserved for
you;
Scarlet experiment! sceptic
Thomas,
    Now, do you doubt that your
bird was true?

VIII.

To lose thee, sweeter than to gain
    All other hearts I knew.
'T is true the drought is destitute,

But then I had the dew!

The Caspian has its realms of sand,
    Its other realm of sea;
Without the sterile perquisite
    No Caspian could be.

IX.

Poor little heart!
    Did they forget thee?
Then dinna care! Then dinna care!

Proud little heart!
    Did they forsake thee?
Be debonair! Be debonair!

Frail little heart!
    I would not break thee:
Could'st credit me? Could'st credit
me?

Gay little heart!
    Like morning glory
Thou'll wilted be; thou'll wilted
be!

X - Forgotten

There is a word
    Which bears a sword
    Can pierce an armed man.
It hurls its barbed syllables,—
    At once is mute again.
But where it fell
The saved will tell
    On patriotic day,
Some epauletted brother
    Gave his breath away.

102

Wherever runs the breathless sun,
  Wherever roams the day,
There is its noiseless onset,
  There is its victory!

Behold the keenest marksman!
  The most accomplished shot!
Time's sublimest target
  Is a soul 'forgot'!

XI.

I've got an arrow here;
  Loving the hand that sent it,
I the dart revere.

Fell, they will say, in 'skirmish'!
  Vanquished, my soul will know,
By but a simple arrow
  Sped by an archer's bow.

XII - The Master

He fumbles at your spirit
  As players at the keys
Before they drop full music on;
  He stuns you by degrees,

Prepares your brittle substance
  For the ethereal blow,
By fainter hammers, further
heard,
  Then nearer, then so slow

Your breath has time to
straighten,
  Your brain to bubble cool, —
Deals one imperial thunderbolt
  That scalps your naked soul.

XIII.

Heart, we will forget him!
  You and I, to-night!
You may forget the warmth he
gave,
  I will forget the light.

When you have done, pray tell me,
  That I my thoughts may dim;
Haste! lest while you're lagging,
  I may remember him!

XIV.

Father, I bring thee not myself, —
  That were the little load;
I bring thee the imperial heart
  I had not strength to hold.

The heart I cherished in my own
  Till mine too heavy grew,
Yet strangest, heavier since it
went,
  Is it too large for you?

XV.

We outgrow love like other things
  And put it in the drawer,
Till it an antique fashion shows
  Like costumes grandsires wore.

XVI.

Not with a club the heart is
broken,
  Nor with a stone;

A whip, so small you could not see
it.
    I've known

To lash the magic creature
    Till it fell,
Yet that whip's name too noble
    Then to tell.

Magnanimous of bird
    By boy descried,
To sing unto the stone
    Of which it died.

XVII - Who?

My friend must be a bird,
    Because it flies!
Mortal my friend must be,
    Because it dies!
Barbs has it, like a bee.
Ah, curious friend,
    Thou puzzlest me!

XVIII.

He touched me, so I live to know
That such a day, permitted so,
    I groped upon his breast.
It was a boundless place to me,
And silenced, as the awful sea
    Puts minor streams to rest.

And now, I'm different from
before,
As if I breathed superior air,
    Or brushed a royal gown;
My feet, too, that had wandered
so,

My gypsy face transfigured now
    To tenderer renown.

XIX - Dreams

Let me not mar that perfect dream
    By an auroral stain,
But so adjust my daily night
    That it will come again.

XX - Numen Lumen

I live with him, I see his face;
    I go no more away
For visitor, or sundown;
    Death's single privacy,

The only one forestalling mine,
    And that by right that he
Presents a claim invisible,
    No wedlock granted me.

I live with him, I hear his voice,
    I stand alive to-day
To witness to the certainty
    Of immortality

Taught me by Time, — the lower
way,
    Conviction every day, —
That life like this is endless,
    Be judgment what it may.

XXI - Longing

I envy seas whereon he rides,
    I envy spokes of wheels
Of chariots that him convey,
    I envy speechless hills

That gaze upon his journey;
  How easy all can see
What is forbidden utterly
  As heaven, unto me!

I envy nests of sparrows
  That dot his distant eaves,
The wealthy fly upon his pane,
  The happy, happy leaves

That just abroad his window
  Have summer's leave to be,
The earrings of Pizarro
  Could not obtain for me.

I envy light that wakes him,
  And bells that boldly ring
To tell him it is noon abroad, —
  Myself his noon could bring,

Yet interdict my blossom
  And abrogate my bee,
Lest noon in everlasting night
  Drop Gabriel and me.

XXII - Wedded

A solemn thing it was, I said,
  A woman white to be,
And wear, if God should count me
fit,
  Her hallowed mystery.

A timid thing to drop a life
  Into the purple well,
Too plummetless that it come
back
  Eternity until.

III. Nature

I - Nature's Changes

The springtime's pallid landscape
  Will glow like bright bouquet,
Though drifted deep in parian
  The village lies to-day.

The lilacs, bending many a year,
  With purple load will hang;
The bees will not forget the tune
  Their old forefathers sang.

The rose will redden in the bog,
  The aster on the hill
Her everlasting fashion set,
  And covenant gentians frill,

Till summer folds her miracle
  As women do their gown,
Or priests adjust the symbols
  When sacrament is done.

II - The Tulip

She slept beneath a tree
  Remembered but by me.
I touched her cradle mute;
  She recognized the foot,
Put on her carmine suit, —
  And see!

III.

A light exists in spring
  Not present on the year
At any other period.

When March is scarcely here
A color stands abroad
  On solitary hills
That science cannot overtake,
  But human nature feels.

It waits upon the lawn;
  It shows the furthest tree
Upon the furthest slope we know;
  It almost speaks to me.

Then, as horizons step,
  Or noons report away,
Without the formula of sound,
  It passes, and we stay:

A quality of loss
  Affecting our content,
As trade had suddenly encroached
  Upon a sacrament.

IV - The Waking Year

A lady red upon the hill
  Her annual secret keeps;
A lady white within the field
  In placid lily sleeps!

The tidy breezes with their
brooms
  Sweep vale, and hill, and tree!
Prithee, my pretty housewives!
  Who may expected be?

The neighbors do not yet suspect!
  The woods exchange a smile —
Orchard, and buttercup, and bird
—
  In such a little while!

And yet how still the landscape
stands,
  How nonchalant the wood,
As if the resurrection
  Were nothing very odd!

V - To March

Dear March, come in!
How glad I am!
I looked for you before.
Put down your hat —
You must have walked —
How out of breath you are!
Dear March, how are you?
And the rest?
Did you leave Nature well?
Oh, March, come right upstairs
with me,
I have so much to tell!

I got your letter, and the birds';
The maples never knew
That you were coming, — I
declare,
How red their faces grew!
But, March, forgive me —
And all those hills
You left for me to hue;
There was no purple suitable,
You took it all with you.

Who knocks? That April!
Lock the door!
I will not be pursued!
He stayed away a year, to call
When I am occupied.
But trifles look so trivial
As soon as you have come,

That blame is just as dear as
praise
And praise as mere as blame.

VI - March

We like March, his shoes are
purple,
  He is new and high;
Makes he mud for dog and
peddler,
  Makes he forest dry;
Knows the adder's tongue his
coming,
  And begets her spot.
Stands the sun so close and mighty
  That our minds are hot.
News is he of all the others;
  Bold it were to die
With the blue-birds buccaneering
  On his British sky.

VII - Dawn

Not knowing when the dawn will
come
  I open every door;
Or has it feathers like a bird,
  Or billows like a shore?

VIII.

A murmur in the trees to note,
  Not loud enough for wind;
A star not far enough to seek,
  Nor near enough to find;

A long, long yellow on the lawn,
  A hubbub as of feet;

Not audible, as ours to us,
　But dapperer, more sweet;

A hurrying home of little men
　To houses unperceived, —
All this, and more, if I should tell,
　Would never be believed.

Of robins in the trundle bed
　How many I espy
Whose nightgowns could not hide
the wings,
　Although I heard them try!

But then I promised ne'er to tell;
　How could I break my word?
So go your way and I'll go mine, —
　No fear you'll miss the road.

IX.

Morning is the place for dew,
　Corn is made at noon,
After dinner light for flowers,
　Dukes for setting sun!

X.

To my quick ear the leaves
conferred;
　The bushes they were bells;
I could not find a privacy
　From Nature's sentinels.

In cave if I presumed to hide,
　The walls began to tell;
Creation seemed a mighty crack
　To make me visible.

XI - A Rose

A sepal, petal, and a thorn
　Upon a common summer's morn,
A flash of dew, a bee or two,
A breeze
A caper in the trees, —
　And I'm a rose!

XII.

High from the earth I heard a bird;
　He trod upon the trees
As he esteemed them trifles,
　And then he spied a breeze,
And situated softly
　Upon a pile of wind
Which in a perturbation
　Nature had left behind.
A joyous-going fellow
　I gathered from his talk,
Which both of benediction
　And badinage partook,
Without apparent burden,
　I learned, in leafy wood
He was the faithful father
　Of a dependent brood;
And this untoward transport
　His remedy for care, —
A contrast to our respites.
　How different we are!

XIII - Cobwebs

The spider as an artist
　Has never been employed
Though his surpassing merit
　Is freely certified

By every broom and Bridget
  Throughout a Christian land.
Neglected son of genius,
  I take thee by the hand.

XIV - A Well

What mystery pervades a well!
  The water lives so far,
Like neighbor from another world
  Residing in a jar.

The grass does not appear afraid;
  I often wonder he
Can stand so close and look so
bold
  At what is dread to me.

Related somehow they may be, —
  The sedge stands next the sea,
Where he is floorless, yet of fear
  No evidence gives he.

But nature is a stranger yet;
  The ones that cite her most
Have never passed her haunted
house,
  Nor simplified her ghost.

To pity those that know her not
  Is helped by the regret
That those who know her, know
her less
  The nearer her they get.

XV.

To make a prairie it takes a clover
and one bee, —

One clover, and a bee,
And revery.
The revery alone will do
If bees are few.

XVI - The Wind

It's like the light, —
  A fashionless delight
It's like the bee, —
  A dateless melody.

It's like the woods,
  Private like breeze,
Phraseless, yet it stirs
  The proudest trees.

It's like the morning, —
  Best when it's done, —
The everlasting clocks
  Chime noon.

XVII.

A dew sufficed itself
  And satisfied a leaf,
And felt, 'how vast a destiny!
  How trivial is life!'

The sun went out to work,
  The day went out to play,
But not again that dew was seen
  By physiognomy.

Whether by day abducted,
  Or emptied by the sun
Into the sea, in passing,
  Eternally unknown.

XVIII - The Woodpecker

His bill an auger is,
  His head, a cap and frill.
He laboreth at every tree, —
  A worm his utmost goal.

XIX - A Snake.

Sweet is the swamp with its
secrets,
  Until we meet a snake;
'T is then we sigh for houses,
  And our departure take
At that enthralling gallop
  That only childhood knows.
A snake is summer's treason,
  And guile is where it goes.

XX.

Could I but ride indefinite,
  As doth the meadow-bee,
And visit only where I liked,
  And no man visit me,

And flirt all day with buttercups,
  And marry whom I may,
And dwell a little everywhere,
  Or better, run away

With no police to follow,
  Or chase me if I do,
Till I should jump peninsulas
  To get away from you, —

I said, but just to be a bee
  Upon a raft of air,
And row in nowhere all day long,

And anchor off the bar,—
What liberty! So captives deem
Who tight in dungeons are.

XXI - The Moon

The moon was but a chin of gold
  A night or two ago,
And now she turns her perfect
face
  Upon the world below.

Her forehead is of amplest blond;
  Her cheek like beryl stone;
Her eye unto the summer dew
  The likest I have known.

Her lips of amber never part;
  But what must be the smile
Upon her friend she could bestow
  Were such her silver will!

And what a privilege to be
  But the remotest star!
For certainly her way might pass
  Beside your twinkling door.

Her bonnet is the firmament,
  The universe her shoe,
The stars the trinkets at her belt,
  Her dimities of blue.

XXII - The Bat

The bat is dun with wrinkled
wings
  Like fallow article,
And not a song pervades his lips,
  Or none perceptible.

His small umbrella, quaintly
halved,
   Describing in the air
An arc alike inscrutable, —
   Elate philosopher!

Deputed from what firmament
   Of what astute abode,
Empowered with what
malevolence
   Auspiciously withheld.

To his adroit Creator
   Ascribe no less the praise;
Beneficent, believe me,
   His eccentricities.

XXIII - The Balloon

You've seen balloons set, haven't
you?
   So stately they ascend
It is as swans discarded you
   For duties diamond.

Their liquid feet go softly out
   Upon a sea of blond;
They spurn the air as 't were too
mean
   For creatures so renowned.

Their ribbons just beyond the eye,
   They struggle some for breath,
And yet the crowd applauds
below;
   They would not encore death.

The gilded creature strains and
spins,
   Trips frantic in a tree,

Tears open her imperial veins
   And tumbles in the sea.

The crowd retire with an oath
   The dust in streets goes down,
And clerks in counting-rooms
observe,
   ''T was only a balloon.'

XXIV - Evening

The cricket sang,
And set the sun,
And workmen finished, one by
one,
   Their seam the day upon.

The low grass loaded with the
dew,
The twilight stood as strangers do
With hat in hand, polite and new,
   To stay as if, or go.

A vastness, as a neighbor, came, —
A wisdom without face or name,
A peace, as hemispheres at home,
—
   And so the night became.

XXV - Cocoon

Drab habitation of whom?
Tabernacle or tomb,
Or dome of worm,
Or porch of gnome,
Or some elf's catacomb?

XXVI - Sunset

A sloop of amber slips away
  Upon an ether sea,
And wrecks in peace a purple tar,
  The son of ecstasy.

XXVII - Aurora

Of bronze and blaze
  The north, to-night!
  So adequate its forms,
So preconcerted with itself,
  So distant to alarms, —
An unconcern so sovereign
  To universe, or me,
It paints my simple spirit
  With tints of majesty,
Till I take vaster attitudes,
  And strut upon my stem,
Disdaining men and oxygen,
  For arrogance of them.

My splendors are menagerie;
  But their competeless show
Will entertain the centuries
  When I am, long ago,
An island in dishonored grass,
  Whom none but daisies know.

XXVIII - The Coming Of Night

How the old mountains drip with
sunset,
  And the brake of dun!
How the hemlocks are tipped in
tinsel
  By the wizard sun!

How the old steeples hand the
scarlet,
  Till the ball is full, —
Have I the lip of the flamingo
  That I dare to tell?

Then, how the fire ebbs like
billows,
  Touching all the grass
With a departing, sapphire
feature,
  As if a duchess pass!

How a small dusk crawls on the
village
  Till the houses blot;
And the odd flambeaux no men
carry
  Glimmer on the spot!

Now it is night in nest and kennel,
  And where was the wood,
Just a dome of abyss is nodding
  Into solitude! —

These are the visions baffled
Guido;
  Titian never told;
Domenichino dropped the pencil,
  Powerless to unfold.

XXIX - Aftermath

The murmuring of bees has
ceased;
  But murmuring of some
Posterior, prophetic,
  Has simultaneous come, —

The lower metres of the year,

When nature's laugh is done, —
The Revelations of the book
  Whose Genesis is June.

IV. Time And Eternity

I.

This world is not conclusion;
  A sequel stands beyond,
Invisible, as music,
  But positive, as sound.
It beckons and it baffles;
  Philosophies don't know,
And through a riddle, at the last,
  Sagacity must go.
To guess it puzzles scholars;
  To gain it, men have shown
Contempt of generations,
  And crucifixion known.

II.

We learn in the retreating
  How vast an one
Was recently among us.
  A perished sun

Endears in the departure
  How doubly more
Than all the golden presence
  It was before!

III.

They say that 'time assuages,' —
  Time never did assuage;
An actual suffering strengthens,
  As sinews do, with age.

Time is a test of trouble,
  But not a remedy.
If such it prove, it prove too
  There was no malady.

IV.

We cover thee, sweet face.
  Not that we tire of thee,
But that thyself fatigue of us;
  Remember, as thou flee,
We follow thee until
  Thou notice us no more,
And then, reluctant, turn away
  To con thee o'er and o'er,
And blame the scanty love
  We were content to show,
Augmented, sweet, a hundred fold
  If thou would'st take it now.

V - Ending

That is solemn we have ended, —
  Be it but a play,
Or a glee among the garrets,
  Or a holiday,

Or a leaving home; or later,
  Parting with a world
We have understood, for better
  Still it be unfurled.

VI.

The stimulus, beyond the grave
  His countenance to see,
Supports me like imperial drams
  Afforded royally.

VII.

Given in marriage unto thee,
  Oh, thou celestial host!
Bride of the Father and the Son,
  Bride of the Holy Ghost!

Other betrothal shall dissolve,
  Wedlock of will decay;
Only the keeper of this seal
  Conquers mortality.

VIII.

That such have died enables us
  The tranquiller to die;
That such have lived, certificate
  For immortality.

IX.

They won't frown always, — some
sweet day
  When I forget to tease,
They'll recollect how cold I looked,
  And how I just said 'please.'

Then they will hasten to the door
  To call the little child,
Who cannot thank them, for the
ice
  That on her lisping piled.

X - Immortality

It is an honorable thought,
  And makes one lift one's hat,
As one encountered gentlefolk

Upon a daily street,

That we've immortal place,
  Though pyramids decay,
And kingdoms, like the orchard,
  Flit russetly away.

XI.

The distance that the dead have
gone
  Does not at first appear;
Their coming back seems possible
  For many an ardent year.

And then, that we have followed
them
  We more than half suspect,
So intimate have we become
  With their dear retrospect.

XII.

How dare the robins sing,
  When men and women hear
Who since they went to their
account
  Have settled with the year! —
Paid all that life had earned
  In one consummate bill,
And now, what life or death can do
  Is immaterial.
Insulting is the sun
  To him whose mortal light,
Beguiled of immortality,
  Bequeaths him to the night.
In deference to him
  Extinct be every hum,

Whose garden wrestles with the
dew,
 At daybreak overcome!

XIII - Death

Death is like the insect
 Menacing the tree,
Competent to kill it,
 But decoyed may be.

Bait it with the balsam,
 Seek it with the knife,
Baffle, if it cost you
 Everything in life.

Then, if it have burrowed
 Out of reach of skill,
Ring the tree and leave it, —
 'T is the vermin's will.

XIV - Unwarned

'T is sunrise, little maid, hast thou
 No station in the day?
'T was not thy wont to hinder so,
—
 Retrieve thine industry.

'T is noon, my little maid, alas!
 And art thou sleeping yet?
The lily waiting to be wed,
 The bee, dost thou forget?

My little maid, 't is night; alas,
 That night should be to thee
Instead of morning! Hadst thou
broached
 Thy little plan to me,

Dissuade thee if I could not, sweet,
 I might have aided thee.

XV.

Each that we lose takes part of us;
 A crescent still abides,
Which like the moon, some turbid
night,
 Is summoned by the tides.

XVI.

Not any higher stands the grave
 For heroes than for men;
Not any nearer for the child
 Than numb three-score and ten.

This latest leisure equal lulls
 The beggar and his queen;
Propitiate this democrat
 By summer's gracious mien.

XVII - Asleep

As far from pity as complaint,
 As cool to speech as stone,
As numb to revelation
 As if my trade were bone.

As far from time as history,
 As near yourself to-day
As children to the rainbow's scarf,
 Or sunset's yellow play

To eyelids in the sepulchre.
 How still the dancer lies,
While color's revelations break,
 And blaze the butterflies!

XVIII - The Spirit

'T is whiter than an Indian pipe,
  'T is dimmer than a lace;
No stature has it, like a fog,
  When you approach the place.

Not any voice denotes it here,
  Or intimates it there;
A spirit, how doth it accost?
  What customs hath the air?

This limitless hyperbole
  Each one of us shall be;
'T is drama, if (hypothesis)
  It be not tragedy!

XIX - The Monument

She laid her docile crescent down,
  And this mechanic stone
Still states, to dates that have
forgot,
  The news that she is gone.

So constant to its stolid trust,
  The shaft that never knew,
It shames the constancy that fled
  Before its emblem flew.

XX.

Bless God, he went as soldiers,
  His musket on his breast;
Grant, God, he charge the bravest
  Of all the martial blest.

Please God, might I behold him
  In epauletted white,

I should not fear the foe then,
  I should not fear the fight.

XXI.

Immortal is an ample word
  When what we need is by,
But when it leaves us for a time,
  'T is a necessity.

Of heaven above the firmest proof
  We fundamental know,
Except for its marauding hand,
  It had been heaven below.

XXII.

Where every bird is bold to go,
  And bees abashless play,
The foreigner before he knocks
  Must thrust the tears away.

XXIII.

The grave my little cottage is,
  Where, keeping house for thee,
I make my parlor orderly,
  And lay the marble tea,

For two divided, briefly,
  A cycle, it may be,
Till everlasting life unite
  In strong society.

XXIV.

This was in the white of the year,
  That was in the green,

Drifts were as difficult then to
think
  As daisies now to be seen.

Looking back is best that is left,
  Or if it be before,
Retrospection is prospect's half,
  Sometimes almost more.

XXV.

Sweet hours have perished here;
  This is a mighty room;
Within its precincts hopes have
played, —
  Now shadows in the tomb.

XXVI.

Me! Come! My dazzled face
In such a shining place!

Me! Hear! My foreign ear
The sounds of welcome near!

The saints shall meet
Our bashful feet.

My holiday shall be
That they remember me;

My paradise, the fame
That they pronounce my name.

XXVII - Invisible

From us she wandered now a
year,
  Her tarrying unknown;

If wilderness prevent her feet,
  Or that ethereal zone

No eye hath seen and lived,
  We ignorant must be.
We only know what time of year
  We took the mystery.

XXVIII.

I wish I knew that woman's name,
  So, when she comes this way,
To hold my life, and hold my ears,
  For fear I hear her say

She's 'sorry I am dead,' again,
  Just when the grave and I
Have sobbed ourselves almost to
sleep, —
  Our only lullaby.

XXIX - Trying To Forget

Bereaved of all, I went abroad,
  No less bereaved to be
Upon a new peninsula, —
  The grave preceded me,

Obtained my lodgings ere myself,
  And when I sought my bed,
The grave it was, reposed upon
  The pillow for my head.

I waked, to find it first awake,
  I rose, — it followed me;
I tried to drop it in the crowd,
  To lose it in the sea,

In cups of artificial drowse

To sleep its shape away, —
The grave was finished, but the spade
  Remained in memory.

XXX.

I felt a funeral in my brain,
  And mourners, to and fro,
Kept treading, treading, till it seemed
  That sense was breaking through.

And when they all were seated,
  A service like a drum
Kept beating, beating, till I thought
  My mind was going numb.

And then I heard them lift a box,
  And creak across my soul
With those same boots of lead, again.
  Then space began to toll

As all the heavens were a bell,
  And Being but an ear,
And I and silence some strange race,
  Wrecked, solitary, here.

XXXI.

I meant to find her when I came;
  Death had the same design;
But the success was his, it seems,
  And the discomfit mine.

I meant to tell her how I longed

For just this single time;
But Death had told her so the first,
  And she had hearkened him.

To wander now is my abode;
  To rest, — to rest would be
A privilege of hurricane
  To memory and me.

XXXII - Waiting

I sing to use the waiting,
  My bonnet but to tie,
And shut the door unto my house;
  No more to do have I,

Till, his best step approaching,
  We journey to the day,
And tell each other how we sang
  To keep the dark away.

XXXIII.

A sickness of this world it most occasions
  When best men die;
A wishfulness their far condition
  To occupy.

A chief indifference, as foreign
  A world must be
Themselves forsake contented,
  For Deity.

XXXIV.

Superfluous were the sun
  When excellence is dead;
He were superfluous every day,

For every day is said

That syllable whose faith
  Just saves it from despair,
And whose 'I'll meet you' hesitates
  If love inquire, 'Where?'

Upon his dateless fame
  Our periods may lie,
As stars that drop anonymous
  From an abundant sky.

XXXV.

So proud she was to die
  It made us all ashamed
That what we cherished, so
unknown
  To her desire seemed.

So satisfied to go
  Where none of us should be,
Immediately, that anguish stooped
  Almost to jealousy.

XXXVI - Farewell

Tie the strings to my life, my Lord,
  Then I am ready to go!
Just a look at the horses —
  Rapid! That will do!

Put me in on the firmest side,
  So I shall never fall;
For we must ride to the Judgment,
  And it's partly down hill.

But never I mind the bridges,
  And never I mind the sea;

Held fast in everlasting race
  By my own choice and thee.

Good-by to the life I used to live,
  And the world I used to know;
And kiss the hills for me, just once;
  Now I am ready to go!

XXXVII.

The dying need but little, dear, —
  A glass of water's all,
A flower's unobtrusive face
  To punctuate the wall,

A fan, perhaps, a friend's regret,
  And certainly that one
No color in the rainbow
  Perceives when you are gone.

XXXVIII - Dead

There's something quieter than
sleep
  Within this inner room!
It wears a sprig upon its breast,
  And will not tell its name.

Some touch it and some kiss it,
  Some chafe its idle hand;
It has a simple gravity
  I do not understand!

While simple-hearted neighbors
  Chat of the 'early dead,'
We, prone to periphrasis,
  Remark that birds have fled!

XXXIX.

The soul should always stand ajar,
  That if the heaven inquire,
He will not be obliged to wait,
  Or shy of troubling her.

Depart, before the host has slid
  The bolt upon the door,
To seek for the accomplished
guest, —
  Her visitor no more.

XL.

Three weeks passed since I had
seen her, —
  Some disease had vexed;
'T was with text and village
singing
  I beheld her next,

And a company — our pleasure
  To discourse alone;
Gracious now to me as any,
  Gracious unto none.

Borne, without dissent of either,
  To the parish night;
Of the separated people
  Which are out of sight?

XLI.

I breathed enough to learn the
trick,
  And now, removed from air,
I simulate the breath so well,
  That one, to be quite sure

The lungs are stirless, must
descend
  Among the cunning cells,
And touch the pantomime himself.
  How cool the bellows feels!

XLII.

I wonder if the sepulchre
  Is not a lonesome way,
When men and boys, and larks
and June
  Go down the fields to hay!

XLIII - Joy In Death

If tolling bell I ask the cause.
  'A soul has gone to God,'
I'm answered in a lonesome tone;
  Is heaven then so sad?

That bells should joyful ring to tell
  A soul had gone to heaven,
Would seem to me the proper way
  A good news should be given.

XLIV.

If I may have it when it's dead
  I will contented be;
If just as soon as breath is out
  It shall belong to me,

Until they lock it in the grave,
  'T is bliss I cannot weigh,
For though they lock thee in the
grave,
  Myself can hold the key.

Think of it, lover! I and thee
   Permitted face to face to be;
After a life, a death we'll say, —
   For death was that, and this is
thee.

XLV.

Before the ice is in the pools,
   Before the skaters go,
Or any cheek at nightfall
   Is tarnished by the snow,

Before the fields have finished,
   Before the Christmas tree,
Wonder upon wonder
   Will arrive to me!

What we touch the hems of
   On a summer's day;
What is only walking
   Just a bridge away;

That which sings so, speaks so,
   When there's no one here, —
Will the frock I wept in
   Answer me to wear?

XLVI - Dying

I heard a fly buzz when I died;
   The stillness round my form
Was like the stillness in the air
   Between the heaves of storm.

The eyes beside had wrung them
dry,
   And breaths were gathering sure
For that last onset, when the king

Be witnessed in his power.

I willed my keepsakes, signed
away
   What portion of me I
Could make assignable, — and
then
   There interposed a fly,

With blue, uncertain, stumbling
buzz,
   Between the light and me;
And then the windows failed, and
then
   I could not see to see.

XLVII.

Adrift! A little boat adrift!
   And night is coming down!
Will no one guide a little boat
   Unto the nearest town?

So sailors say, on yesterday,
   Just as the dusk was brown,
One little boat gave up its strife,
   And gurgled down and down.

But angels say, on yesterday,
   Just as the dawn was red,
One little boat o'erspent with
gales
Retrimmed its masts, redecked its
sails
   Exultant, onward sped!

XLVIII.

There's been a death in the
opposite house

122

As lately as to-day.
I know it by the numb look
  Such houses have alway.

The neighbors rustle in and out,
  The doctor drives away.
A window opens like a pod,
  Abrupt, mechanically;

Somebody flings a mattress out, —
  The children hurry by;
They wonder if It died on that, —
  I used to when a boy.

The minister goes stiffly in
  As if the house were his,
And he owned all the mourners now,
  And little boys besides;

And then the milliner, and the man
  Of the appalling trade,
To take the measure of the house.
  There'll be that dark parade

Of tassels and of coaches soon;
  It's easy as a sign, —
The intuition of the news
  In just a country town.

XLIX.

We never know we go, — when we are going
  We jest and shut the door;
Fate following behind us bolts it,
  And we accost no more.

L - The Soul's Storm

It struck me every day
  The lightning was as new
As if the cloud that instant slit
  And let the fire through.

It burned me in the night,
  It blistered in my dream;
It sickened fresh upon my sight
  With every morning's beam.

I thought that storm was brief, —
  The maddest, quickest by;
But Nature lost the date of this,
  And left it in the sky.

LI.

Water is taught by thirst;
Land, by the oceans passed;
  Transport, by throe;
Peace, by its battles told;
Love, by memorial mould;
  Birds, by the snow.

LII - Thirst

We thirst at first, — 't is Nature's act;
  And later, when we die,
A little water supplicate
  Of fingers going by.

It intimates the finer want,
  Whose adequate supply
Is that great water in the west
  Termed immortality.

LIII.

A clock stopped — not the
mantel's;
  Geneva's farthest skill
Can't put the puppet bowing
  That just now dangled still.

An awe came on the trinket!
  The figures hunched with pain,
Then quivered out of decimals
  Into degreeless noon.

It will not stir for doctors,
  This pendulum of snow;
The shopman importunes it,
  While cool, concernless No

Nods from the gilded pointers,
  Nods from the seconds slim,
Decades of arrogance between
  The dial life and him.

LIV - Charlotte Brontë's Grave

All overgrown by cunning moss,
  All interspersed with weed,
The little cage of 'Currer Bell,'
  In quiet Haworth laid.

This bird, observing others,
  When frosts too sharp became,
Retire to other latitudes,
  Quietly did the same,

But differed in returning;
  Since Yorkshire hills are green,
Yet not in all the nests I meet
  Can nightingale be seen.

Gathered from many wanderings,
  Gethsemane can tell
Through what transporting
anguish
  She reached the asphodel!

Soft fall the sounds of Eden
  Upon her puzzled ear;
Oh, what an afternoon for heaven,
  When 'Brontë' entered there!

LV.

A toad can die of light!
Death is the common right
  Of toads and men, —
Of earl and midge
The privilege.
  Why swagger then?
The gnat's supremacy
Is large as thine.

LVI.

Far from love the Heavenly Father
  Leads the chosen child;
Oftener through realm of briar
  Than the meadow mild,

Oftener by the claw of dragon
  Than the hand of friend,
Guides the little one predestined
  To the native land.

LVII - Sleeping

A long, long sleep, a famous sleep
  That makes no show for dawn

By stretch of limb or stir of lid, —
  An independent one.

Was ever idleness like this?
  Within a hut of stone
To bask the centuries away
  Nor once look up for noon?

But this sort grieved myself, and so
  I thought how it would be
When just this time, some perfect year,
    Themselves should come to me.

LVIII - Retrospect

'T was just this time last year I died.
  I know I heard the corn,
When I was carried by the farms, —
  It had the tassels on.

I thought how yellow it would look
  When Richard went to mill;
And then I wanted to get out,
  But something held my will.

I thought just how red apples wedged
  The stubble's joints between;
And carts went stooping round the fields
  To take the pumpkins in.

I wondered which would miss me least,
  And when Thanksgiving came,
If father'd multiply the plates
  To make an even sum.

And if my stocking hung too high,
  Would it blur the Christmas glee,
That not a Santa Claus could reach
  The altitude of me?

LIX - Eternity

On this wondrous sea,
Sailing silently,
  Ho! pilot, ho!
Knowest thou the shore
Where no breakers roar,
  Where the storm is o'er?

In the silent west
Many sails at rest,
  Their anchors fast;
Thither I pilot thee, —
Land, ho! Eternity!
  Ashore at last!

Index of First Lines

Death is like the insect
Death sets a thing significant
Delayed till she had ceased to know,
Delight becomes pictorial
Departed to the judgment,
Did the harebell loose her girdle
Doubt me, my dim companion!
Drab habitation of whom?
Drowning is not so pitiful
Each life converges to some centre
Each that we lose takes part of us;
Elysium is as far as to
Essential oils are wrung:
Except the heaven had come so near,
Except to heaven, she is nought;
Experiment to me
Exultation is the going
Far from love the Heavenly Father
Farther in summer than the birds,
Fate slew him, but he did not drop;
Father, I bring thee not myself, —
Few get enough, — enough is one;
Finite to fail, but infinite to venture.
For each ecstatic instant
Forbidden fruit a flavor has
Frequently the woods are pink,
From all the jails the boys and girls
From cocoon forth a butterfly
From us she wandered now a year,
Given in marriage unto thee,
Glee! The great storm is over!
God gave a loaf to every bird,
God made a little gentian;
God permits industrious angels
Going to heaven!

"Going to him! Happy letter! Tell him —
Good night! which put the candle out?
Great streets of silence led away
Have you got a brook in your little heart,
He ate and drank the precious words,
He fumbles at your spirit
He preached upon "breadth" till it argued him narrow, —
He put the belt around my life, —
He touched me, so I live to know
Heart not so heavy as mine,
Heart, we will forget him!
Heaven is what I cannot reach!
Her final summer was it,
High from the earth I heard a bird;
His bill an auger is,
Hope is a subtle glutton;
Hope is the thing with feathers
How dare the robins sing,
How happy is the little stone
How many times these low feet staggered,
How still the bells in steeples stand,
How the old mountains drip with sunset,
I asked no other thing,
I breathed enough to learn the trick,
I bring an unaccustomed wine
I can wade grief,
I cannot live with you,
I died for beauty, but was scarce
I dreaded that first robin so,
I envy seas whereon he rides,
I felt a clearing in my mind
I felt a funeral in my brain,

I found the phrase to every
thought
I gained it so,
I gave myself to him,
I had a daily bliss
I had a guinea golden;
I had been hungry all the years;
I had no cause to be awake,
I had no time to hate, because
I have a king who does not speak;
I have no life but this,
I have not told my garden yet,
I heard a fly buzz when I died;
I held a jewel in my fingers
I hide myself within my flower,
I know a place where summer
strives
I know some lonely houses off the
road
I know that he exists
I like a look of agony,
I like to see it lap the miles,
I live with him, I see his face;
I lived on dread; to those who
know
I lost a world the other day.
I many times thought peace had
come,
I meant to find her when I came;
I meant to have but modest needs,
I measure every grief I meet
I never hear the word "escape"
I never lost as much but twice,
I never saw a moor,
I noticed people disappeared,
I read my sentence steadily,
I reason, earth is short,
I shall know why, when time is
over,
I should have been too glad, I see,

I should not dare to leave my
friend,
I sing to use the waiting,
I started early, took my dog,
I stepped from plank to plank
I taste a liquor never brewed,
I think just how my shape will rise
I think the hemlock likes to stand
I took my power in my hand.
I went to heaven, —
I went to thank her,
I wish I knew that woman's name,
I wonder if the sepulchre
I worked for chaff, and earning
wheat
I years had been from home,
I'll tell you how the sun rose, —
I'm ceded, I've stopped being
theirs;
I'm nobody! Who are you?
I'm wife; I've finished that,
I've got an arrow here;
I've seen a dying eye
If I can stop one heart from
breaking,
If I may have it when it's dead
If I should die,
If I shouldn't be alive
If anybody's friend be dead,
If recollecting were forgetting,
If the foolish call them 'flowers,'
If tolling bell I ask the cause.
If you were coming in the fall,
Immortal is an ample word
In lands I never saw, they say,
Is Heaven a physician?
Is bliss, then, such abyss
It can't be summer, — that got
through;
It dropped so low in my regard
It is an honorable thought,

It makes no difference abroad,
It might be easier
It sifts from leaden sieves,
It sounded as if the streets were running,
It struck me every day
It tossed and tossed, —
It was not death, for I stood up,
It was too late for man,
It's like the light, —
It's such a little thing to weep,
Just lost when I was saved!
Lay this laurel on the one
Let down the bars, O Death!
Let me not mar that perfect dream
Life, and Death, and Giants
Like mighty footlights burned the red
Like trains of cars on tracks of plush
Look back on time with kindly eyes,
Love is anterior to life,
Me! Come! My dazzled face
Mine by the right of the white election!
Mine enemy is growing old, —
Morning is the place for dew,
Morns like these we parted;
Much madness is divinest sense
Musicians wrestle everywhere:
My cocoon tightens, colors tease,
My country need not change her gown,
My friend must be a bird,
My life closed twice before its close;
My river runs to thee:
My worthiness is all my doubt,
Nature rarer uses yellow
Nature, the gentlest mother,

New feet within my garden go,
No brigadier throughout the year
No rack can torture me,
Not any higher stands the grave
Not in this world to see his face
Not knowing when the dawn will come
Not with a club the heart is broken,
Of all the souls that stand create
Of all the sounds despatched abroad,
Of bronze and blaze
Of tribulation these are they
On such a night, or such a night,
On the bleakness of my lot
On this long storm the rainbow rose,
On this wondrous sea,
One blessing had I, than the rest
One day is there of the series
One dignity delays for all,
One need not be a chamber to be haunted,
One of the ones that Midas touched,
Our journey had advanced;
Our lives are Swiss, —
Our share of night to bear,
Pain has an element of blank;
Perhaps you'd like to buy a flower?
Pigmy seraphs gone astray,
Pink, small, and punctual,
Pompless no life can pass away;
Poor little heart!
Portraits are to daily faces
Prayer is the little implement
Presentiment is that long shadow on the lawn

Proud of my broken heart since
thou didst break it,
Read, sweet, how others strove,
Remembrance has a rear and
front, —
Remorse is memory awake,
Safe in their alabaster chambers,
She died, — this was the way she
died;
She laid her docile crescent down,
She rose to his requirement,
dropped
She slept beneath a tree
She sweeps with many-colored
brooms,
She went as quiet as the dew
Sleep is supposed to be,
So bashful when I spied her,
So proud she was to die
Softened by Time's consummate
plush,
Some keep the Sabbath going to
church;
Some rainbow coming from the
fair!
Some things that fly there be, —
Some, too fragile for winter winds,
Soul, wilt thou toss again?
South winds jostle them,
Split the lark and you'll find the
music,
Step lightly on this narrow spot!
Success is counted sweetest
Summer for thee grant I may be
Superfluous were the sun
Superiority to fate
Surgeons must be very careful
Sweet hours have perished here;
Sweet is the swamp with its
secrets,
Taken from men this morning,

Talk with prudence to a beggar
That I did always love,
That is solemn we have ended, —
That short, potential stir
That such have died enables us
The bat is dun with wrinkled
wings
The bee is not afraid of me,
The body grows outside, —
The bone that has no marrow;
The brain is wider than the sky,
The brain within its groove
The bustle in a house
The butterfly's assumption-gown,
The clouds their backs together
laid,
The cricket sang,
The daisy follows soft the sun,
The day came slow, till five
o'clock,
The distance that the dead have
gone
The dying need but little, dear, —
The farthest thunder that I heard
The gentian weaves her fringes,
The grass so little has to do, —
The grave my little cottage is,
The heart asks pleasure first,
The last night that she lived,
The leaves, like women,
interchange
The moon is distant from the sea,
The moon was but a chin of gold
The morns are meeker than they
were,
The mountain sat upon the plain
The murmur of a bee
The murmuring of bees has
ceased;
The mushroom is the elf of plants,

The nearest dream recedes, unrealized.
The night was wide, and furnished scant
The one that could repeat the summer day
The only ghost I ever saw
The past is such a curious creature,
The pedigree of honey
The rat is the concisest tenant.
The reticent volcano keeps
The robin is the one
The rose did caper on her cheek,
The show is not the show,
The skies can't keep their secret!
The sky is low, the clouds are mean,
The soul selects her own society,
The soul should always stand ajar,
The soul unto itself
The spider as an artist
The springtime's pallid landscape
The stimulus, beyond the grave
The sun just touched the morning;
The sun kept setting, setting still;
The thought beneath so slight a film
The way I read a letter 's this:
The wind begun to rock the grass
Their height in heaven comforts not,
There came a day at summer's full
There came a wind like a bugle;
There is a flower that bees prefer,
There is a shame of nobleness
There is a word
There is no frigate like a book
There's a certain slant of light,
There's been a death in the opposite house

There's something quieter than sleep
These are the days when birds come back,
They dropped like flakes, they dropped like stars,
They say that 'time assuages,' —
They won't frown always, — some sweet day
This is my letter to the world,
This is the land the sunset washes,
This merit hath the worst, —
This was in the white of the year,
This world is not conclusion;
Though I get home how late, how late!
Three weeks passed since I had seen her, —
Through the straight pass of suffering
'T is so much joy! 'T is so much joy!
'T is sunrise, little maid, hast thou
'T is whiter than an Indian pipe,
Tie the strings to my life, my Lord,
To fight aloud is very brave,
To hang our head ostensibly,
To hear an oriole sing
To help our bleaker parts
To know just how he suffered would be dear;
To learn the transport by the pain,
To lose one's faith surpasses
To lose thee, sweeter than to gain
To make a prairie it takes a clover and one bee, —
To my quick ear the leaves conferred;
To venerate the simple days
Triumph may be of several kinds.
'T is little I could care for pearls

'T was a long parting, but the time
'T was just this time last year I
died.
'T was later when the summer
went
'T was such a little, little boat
Two butterflies went out at noon
Two swimmers wrestled on the
spar
Undue significance a starving man
attaches
Unto my books so good to turn
Upon the gallows hung a wretch,
Victory comes late,
Wait till the majesty of Death
Water is taught by thirst;
We cover thee, sweet face.
We learn in the retreating
We like March, his shoes are
purple,
We never know how high we are
We never know we go, — when
we are going
We outgrow love like other things
We play at paste,
We thirst at first, — 't is Nature's
act;
Went up a year this evening!
What if I say I shall not wait?
What inn is this
What mystery pervades a well!
What soft, cherubic creatures
When I hoped I feared,
When I was small, a woman died.
When night is almost done,
When roses cease to bloom, dear,
Where every bird is bold to go,
Where ships of purple gently toss
Whether my bark went down at
sea,
While I was fearing it, it came,

Who has not found the heaven
below
Who never lost, are unprepared
Who never wanted, — maddest
joy
Who robbed the woods,
"Whose are the little beds," I
asked,
Wild nights! Wild nights!
Will there really be a morning?
Within my reach!
You cannot put a fire out;
You left me, sweet, two legacies,
—
You've seen balloons set, haven't
you?
Your riches taught me poverty.

CPSIA information can be obtained
at www.ICGtesting.com
Printed in the USA
LVHW081749121118
596818LV00039B/1644/P

9 781540 408013